DEDICATION

This book is dedicated to
Philip A. Hannema
who created one of the first books on the subject.

---

*"In the words and deeds of the past there lies
hidden a treasure that people may use to
strengthen and elevate their own character."*

—I Ching

Acknowledgements

First of all, thanks to the hundreds of people whose "two bits worth" is found within these pages. Without them this book could not exist. More specifically, thanks to: Rochelle Gatlin who smoothed out much of this edition; Eleanor Vincent who made the first edition look like a real book; Kevin and Rebecca Dwan of Dwan Typography, Sebastopol, CA; Linda Gilligan for a great cover; Cathi Elledge-Gall, Ygnacio Valley High School, Concord, CA, Class of '68; Don Gillingham, Hudson's Bay High School, Vancouver, WA, Class of '60; Fred Jossy, Eagle Point High School, Eagle Point, OR, Class of '59; Howard Thompson, Hayward High School, Hayward, CA, Classes of '52–'55; Craig Stewart, Lakeside School, Seattle, WA; Deborah L. Downey, Director of Special Events and Alumni Services, Antioch University, Yellow Springs, OH; Joe Condrill of Overseas Brats; Herb Reith, Ralph Roberts and Jim Horn for their help with the telecommunications section; and to Tom Crawford and Sid Johnston of The Mosquito Association, who are further acknowledged in Chapter 12.

How to Use This Book

The information and ideas in this book have been collected from organizers of all types of reunions: urban and rural; large and small; simple and elaborate; school, military and family. For this reason, you will find here much more material than you will need for your specific reunion. Therefore, to simplify things we suggest these tips:

- **Use a highlighting pen or colored ink to mark ideas and sections that pertain to your reunion.** One or two of you on the committee should go through this book BEFORE the first meeting and mark the parts that seem the most important and that pertain specifically to your reunion. Mark an especially important point with a paper clip. A few extra minutes spent in this way will work wonders at your meetings.

NOTE: If this is a library book, you can order your own book with the order form in the back. Please don't mark up library books.

- **If you are planning a military reunion,** you will notice that most of this book is written for organizers of school reunions. However, 80% of this information will also apply to military reunions. The other 20% is explained in Chapter 12, "Military Reunions," so read that first. Then read the rest of the book, underlining the points that pertain to your situation.

- **If you are looking for information on family reunions,** you will find some here, but you should really have our *Family Reunion Handbook,* available sometime in 1990. Send us your address and we will notify you of its publication.

- **If you are interested in private school reunions,** please read Chapter 13, "Private Schools," first.

- **Overseas American Schools (Department of Defense Dependent Schools and State Department supported schools),** are covered in Chapter 14.

- **If you are considering hiring a commercial reunion organizer** turn to Chapter 15. This might be the way to go if you really don't have time to "do-it-yourself."

In **Appendix A** you will find a listing of all sources and resources (non-military) mentioned in the text, as well as a bibliography of helpful books.

Appendix B is for military reunions. It lists: 1. Publications that will accept reunion notices, 2. Military Locators, 3. Military-related electronic bulletin boards, and 4. Other help and sources.

"Chronology of a Typical High School Reunion" gives you a graphic visual representation of reunion planning. It can be found in the front of Chapter 2.

In 1990 we will be publishing the *Reunion Organizers Directory* —a "yellow pages" of businesses that cater to reunions. Regional as well as nationwide information will be included. If you would like to be notified of its publication, please send us your address.

How You Can Help

This book is the result of many years of collecting information from the general public. We have conducted interviews (in person, by mail, and by phone), collected articles from magazines, clippings from newspapers, gone to other people's reunions, organized our own, taken photographs, and have otherwise gotten under foot in our never-ending quest to make this a more useful book. We revise this book about every three years, and hopefully each edition is a little better and more informative than the last.

You can help. Send us your input. If we use it in our next edition, you will receive special mention PLUS a free (signed) complimentary copy.

Here's what we are looking for:

- New tips and ideas that aren't found in this book (preferably from your own experience).

- Useful criticisms of tips and ideas in this book. Try to present a good argument from your own experience.

- Magazine articles and newspaper clippings on the subject of: school, family, or military reunions, or commercial reunion organizers.

- Fragments or quotes about reunions found within other printed material.

- Addresses of businesses that cater to reunions, such as: commercial reunion organizers, manufacturers of imprinted giftware, facilities and caterers that you have used, photographers, video companies, etc.

- Other books and pamphlets on how to organize reunions.

- Photographs taken at reunions that illustrate any of the points presented in this book. Preferably black-and-white.

- Computer software that is specifically designed for reunion purposes.

- Presentations, speeches, benedictions, and toasts given at reunions.

- Examples of awards and prizes that we haven't covered.

CONTENTS

PART I
Public School Reunions

"High school is closer to the core of the American experience than anything else I can think of."
—Kurt Vonnegut Jr.,
Notes from the High School Underground

Introduction

Humans have a deep impulse to explore the past. It may be as simple as a trip down memory lane when we hear a song by Benny Goodman, the Four Tops or the Beatles; or as complex as a total re-evaluation of our life, an urge to examine it and put it in perspective, to compare it with the lives of others. This is why reunions—getting together with people with whom we have had a shared bond—are so powerful. They call up that urge to remember, relive, re-evaluate. They put us face to face with the past and force us to ask how we have used it to create the present. They are scary and exciting.

These feelings apply to all reunions, but they seem especially to apply to high school reunions which is the focus of Part I of this book. Those of us who went to school together have one common bond—we shared the transition from adolescence to early adulthood. We were all on the threshold of something. We wanted to be adults, whatever that meant. Old roles didn't seem to fit. Many of us moved in expected directions — college, jobs, marriage, kids. Others did not. Some of us changed directions in midstream; an amazing number, in fact. There were career changes, divorces, cross-country moves. Some of us took on the old roles and struggled to make them fit, to make them our own, rather than simply what was expected. But no matter when we graduated from high school, life held its store of surprises. Time and change are the only constants and they happen to all of us.

Reunions are a very special form of time travel. They take us back to a starting point, a point where certain decisions were made, where some roads were chosen and others were not. What roads did our classmates choose? Were they different from our choices? Are those people we haven't seen in all these years happy? What do they look like, how do they act? Will we remember them? Will **they** remember us? Whatever happened to the class clown, the brainy valedictorian, the most popular cheerleader, and the hordes of others we may not remember clearly? Reunions give us a chance to find out. They offer the possibility of satisfying our curiosity. Like a

good novel, they draw us forward with the tantalizing and then ...
and then ... until we arrive and see for ourselves.

Chances are, we are in for some surprises. People look and act
differently. In fact, they probably aren't the same people we remember at all. We may find ourselves engrossed in conversation with
that bore who used to give the dumbest answers in 4th period
English. Or awestruck by that shy, pimply beanpole who has ma-
tured into a confident, attractive woman with a fascinating career.
Everyone will talk about the highpoints of their lives—graduations,
marriages, births, jobs, promotions, travel. But for those who have
developed the art of observing and listening, deeper information is
in store: information that conveys more, lasts longer and adds
meaning to our own lives. The ultimate challenge and reward of
reunions is to be willing to divulge and collect such information.
We all shared a certain time and a culture with its own rituals and
rules. It may have been the most painful time of our lives, or one of
the happiest, but we were in it together. Reunions give us a chance
to share whatever wisdom—or, at least, common sense—we have
accumulated over the years.

Each year nearly 20 million Americans attend more than 120,000
high school reunions. Each reunion represents years of accumulated knowledge and information being handed down. Reunion
Handbook was created to help facilitate this information sharing
process. You will find lots of practical tips on how to make your
reunion inclusive and comfortable for all your classmates, as well
as the basics of how to organize and share the work of staging a
reunion. And, no doubt about it, organizing a reunion is a lot of
work. We also hope you will find it a satisfying way to look at the
past and re-evaluate the present.

CHAPTER I

Basic Tips

You, as a reunion organizer, are a steward of one of life's most important and powerful social events. The underlying rules behind all of your intentions and decisions should be: **Comfort and Hospitality.** Such an approach will provide people with a memorable event, something they can look back on with approval, knowing that someone tried hard to do a good job, AND it will make them look forward to their next reunion.

What, Me Nervous?

Ninety-five percent of all Americans over the age of 28 are invited to a reunion at least once in their life. More than 20 million people in this country attend reunions each year. But as common as these events are, most people will still confess to some apprehension about attending one. Even those who enjoy reunions (such as reunion organizers) can feel nervous about them. Comfort and hospitality are the two things that can best counteract this nervousness.

But what do we mean by comfort? It's not just good food and a place to sit down. It can involve small things like name tags, or big things like music that doesn't drown out conversation. In fact, every single aspect of your reunion can be approached with comfort and hospitality in mind. **The following tips and ideas, all based on this approach, are a general outline of what you will find in this book:**

A Party Atmosphere Is NOT Necessary

The single biggest mistake that reunion organizers make is to try to create a whoop-it-up party atmosphere — as if it were Saturday night at the hottest local bar. This tendency is understandable.

After all, bars and parties are familiar to most of us, and reunions aren't. Unfortunately, an all-out party atmosphere will limit, or entirely cut off, meaningful communication. People simply will not be able to give their full attention to getting re-acquainted with old friends. Loud music and alcohol should be secondary at reunions; it's not that they shouldn't be there, it's just that they shouldn't be emphasized. If you find yourself (or your committee) falling into the familiar party format, remember that the main purpose of reunions is to bring people together. These people haven't been together in years and are eager to see and talk to each other. This in itself is enough. They arrive already excited and don't need to be over-stimulated.

Loud Music and Conversation Don't Mix

Overly loud music is the most common complaint about reunions, and one of the easiest to avoid with a little advanced planning. Remember that people's main interest is to communicate. The biggest need is to talk. The whole gamut from party-style chit-chat to intense conversation is going to take place with or without your interest or help. All you really need to do is provide the setting.

Include Everyone

This requires a fair amount of detective work because you may have to find people who live across the country or half way around the world. But there are ways to make this a fun and interesting enterprise (or at least to find helpers who consider it fun and interesting). In fact, looking for "lost" classmates can get others involved (through the mailers) in a joint project before the reunion, and give them a chance to start re-establishing contacts (if only mentally) before the event. Also, be sure that everyone is "looked for." Just because you don't remember so-and-so, or didn't like him, is no excuse.

The next "tip" shows how people can be unintentionally excluded.

Reunions Take Time to Plan

Three or four months is NOT enough time to plan a good reunion (unless you have a very small group). To do so would undoubtedly exclude some people who would have to make travel and vacation plans far in advance.

Include Last-Minute Arrivals

A few people will be so ambivalent about attending, they will put off the decision until the last minute. There are several things you can do so these last-minute arrivals won't feel awkward or left out.

Name Tags

Perhaps no fear about reunions is greater than the "recognition problem." "What if I don't recognize my old friends or they don't recognize me?" You can minimize uneasiness and embarrassment by providing special name tags that allow people to easily recognize each other. And let it be known (through the mailers) that such a name tag will be provided.

Activity Centers

Display tables or bulletin boards of memorabilia, letters from classmates, a slide show, old movies, etc., are not only interesting, they provide natural gathering points that allow for people to mix more easily.

Serve Snacks and Refreshments Throughout the Evening

People are more comfortable when they have something to do with their hands (like eat). Also, food cushions the effects of alcohol.

Seating

Don't have a head table. Former class officers, the reunion committee, former teachers, and other "dignitaries" need not be singled out in this way. Try to keep everyone on the same level. (A possible exception would be an "honored" teacher or principal). Don't have assigned seating. Allow people to sit where they wish, and to facilitate "mixing," have the "seated" part of the program as short as possible.

Make the Program Mercifully Short

People at reunions have short attention spans because what they really want to do is talk and become re-acquainted. They absolutely will not tolerate long, drawn-out programs. They will simply start talking to each other.

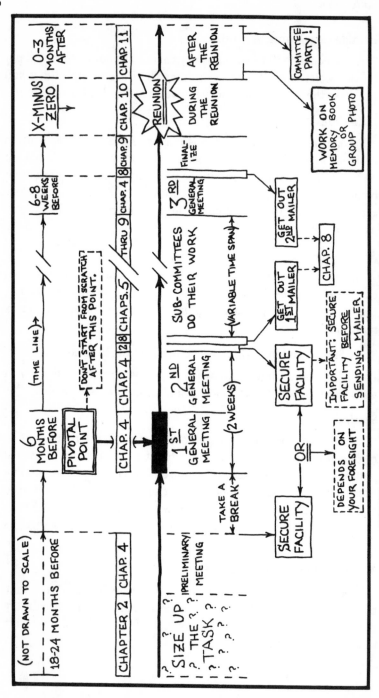

FIGURE 1. A graphic representation of a typical high school reunion.

CHAPTER 2

Early Decisions

Who Makes These Early Decisions? – Is It Time for a Reunion? – What Type of Reunion? – Alternative Types of Reunions – Regional Reunions – Reunions By Mail – How Soon to Reserve a Facility? – Choosing a Facility – When to Have It? – How Much Should You Spend? – A List of Questions to Ask When Talking With the Manager of a Facility.

Who Makes These Early Decisions?

In most cases, a reunion starts with the idea of one person. That person will be faced with making several early decisions. He or she can choose to make these decisions alone, with the help of a few friends, or with the help of a committee. **These decisions all lead to the one factor that must be taken care of before all others: securing a facility.** This chapter deals with these decisions.

Is It Time for a Reunion?

Please excuse the obvious, but the initial decision is whether or not to have a reunion. We mention this because many attempts to organize reunions are aborted due to lack of interest, either within the committee, within the group, or both. And quite often this lack of interest is no one's fault. The need for a reunion is something that builds up within a group over a period of time. If you tap this interest too soon or too often, you can end up with a mediocre event.

We hear this type of complaint a lot:

Organizer: "Our reunion was a dud. What did we do wrong?"

Us: "When was your last reunion?"

Organizer: "Five years ago. Our 25th was so much fun that we thought we'd have a 30th."

The real problem here is in comparing the last two reunions. You can't have a "great" reunion every five years. You can have a "pretty good" reunion; many locals will attend and probably have a good time. But once your group has tasted a "great" reunion, there will always be comparisons, and "time" is the only factor that is going to help. As one reunion organizer put it:

"There's room for only 3 or 4 great reunions in one lifetime."

A reunion is actually a very easy event to make a success. Ultimately you don't really need entertainment, fancy decorations, music, or good food. All you really need is a comfortable place where people can communicate, and a nebulous something, call it "desire" or "need," that only time can provide. A "great" reunion is such a wonderful and rare event in a person's life that we have to recommend about ten years between them. The enthusiasm of the committee can be a good indicator. If there is some doubt, perhaps you should wait awhile for the next reunion. It's better to have a great reunion every ten years than a ho-hum event every five.

What Type of Reunion?

Before you can choose the best place for your reunion, you must be clear about what kind of event your group wants (which may differ from what you want). Most groups, especially those from public schools, are amazingly diverse — economically, socially, ethnically. Try to include as many types of people as possible. Also, different age groups have different tastes. What was great fun for your tenth reunion may not be appropriate for the fortieth.

If you are in doubt about the type of event that would appeal to the greatest number of people, call up (or mail a survey to) a cross-section of your classmates and ask their opinion. Try to make it a representative sampling, not just your old friends. This should at least give you some basic guidelines.

By far the most common type of reunion, especially for up to 30 years after graduation, is the dinner/dance party held in a banquet hall. This is also one of the most expensive. Dinner/dances may be the rule, but what's to say you can't create a more interesting exception? How about a barbeque or picnic at a local park? Potlucks, especially for small groups, are inexpensive and fun. Even a catered buffet can cost less than a sit-down dinner. Any of these alternatives will determine the type of facility you will need which, in turn, will determine the cost. Don't cross out any options until you have had time to discuss the alternatives, visit various facilities, and talk to a cross-section of your classmates. **Remember: The important thing is to provide a comfortable place for people to talk to each other.** Fancy food, a live band, dancing, an entertaining program, etc., are all "extras."

Will alcohol be served? If so, it probably rules out less expensive settings like the school gym, a local church, or some community centers. Some state and local laws allow a one day liquor license to be issued to groups. Running your own bar can be quite lucrative as a fund-raiser.

Are children to be invited? If so, depending on your local and state laws, this may rule out certain facilities (those with liquor bars), or the serving of alcohol in the presence of minors. Some laws draw the line at hard liquor; some at beer and wine.

Outdoor functions will require lights at night as well as restrooms, running water, and plenty of shade for hot summer days.

Alternative Types of Reunions

Regional reunions. This usually happens only with private schools, but occasionally a large public high school will have a regional reunion. It's simply a group of graduates in a regional area (usually a state or large metropolitan area) who have their own little reunion. Most often the participants are from one class, but sometimes all graduates are included. These reunions are often small enough to be held in a private home or a small banquet room in a restaurant. They can be very inexpensive, the only expenses being mailing costs and the meal. (Also see p. 182 in Chapter 13, "Private Schools.")

Reunions by mail. If there is not enough interest or energy to have a reunion, or if your classmates have become too widely scattered to bring them all together at one location, you can have a reunion by mail. One way to do this is to ask classmates to mail biographical information about themselves to a "Reunion Coordinator" (see the end of Chapter 8 for a sample survey form). The coordinator then gathers this material and mails photocopies of the originals out to each class member.

Some classes take this information and create an "alumni newsletter." Frequency of such newsletters varies from "once only" to every six months. They are typed and reproduced by photocopy or "quick printing" processes. The new "desktop publishing" ability of some personal computers can produce amazing results, but of course a certain amount of money and expertise is required. See Chapter 8 for more details.

Another variation is to have a "Christmas card reunion." Classmates send Christmas greetings or letters to one individual by a certain set date. These greetings and letters are then put together, copied, and sent to all classmates. Remember that blue ink may not photocopy well. Most copy machines are designed to not "see" the color blue, although there are exceptions. Either find a copy machine that can copy blue, or ask your correspondents to write in black or red ink (red will photocopy as black).

A "round robin letter" works well with very small groups—about 15 participants is the maximum. One person starts it off by writing a letter to everyone, enclosing an address list of all participants and a short explanation, and mailing all of this to the first person on the mailing list, putting his or her own name at the bottom. The next person writes a letter, perhaps commenting on the enclosed letters, and sends the whole batch on to the next person. And so it goes until interest wanes, but chances are good that it will make it through at least one complete round. It's a good idea to set a deadline on the responding time—say 3 to 4 weeks per person—and to allow the participants to add others onto the mailing list if they so desire. Also mention that if a person doesn't want to respond that he or she should feel all right about just sending it on to the next person. That way it won't get "hung up" so often.

Like other types of reunions, reunions by mail are financed by donations from classmates. You may need to solicit for this.

How Soon to Reserve a Facility?

Securing a facility (putting down non-refundable money and signing a contract) represents the point of no return in reunion organizing. Until then you don't really have a reunion happening. Afterward, however, you are "in for the ride," unless you don't mind loosing your deposit.

The necessity of reserving a facility EARLY often catches people by surprise. Because places that can accommodate reunions are usually in high demand, reservations must be made from 6 to 18 months ahead of time, depending on circumstances. Twelve months ahead is the norm. At six months you are taking your chances, and in some large metropolitan areas 18 months may not be too soon, especially if you would like a particular facility and date.

If you are lucky enough to have secured a facility more than six months before your reunion, then you can take a break. Most other aspects of a reunion can be accomplished in six months. We don't recommend that a reunion be attempted in any less time than this. Three or four months is just not enough time (unless your group is very small and relatively local) because you will wind up either excluding many of those who must travel, or making it more difficult for them to be there. For some people, traveling to a reunion can be a major undertaking, because of kids and taking off time from work. The considerate thing to do would be to give these people at least 6 months notice—more would be nice.

Choosing a Facility

If you opt for the traditional dinner/dance, be aware of the various types of facilities available. Most banquet rooms are located in restaurants and hotels, but other types of facilities—country clubs, fraternal lodges, horse racing facilities—have their own "working kitchens." Such places usually require that you purchase the meal from them. Other facilities — Grange Halls, community centers, and churches — may simply provide a room where you can have your own pot-luck, buffet, or outside caterer. Each place has its own rules. To learn them, take notes and have a list of questions to ask. Such a list can be found in the back of this chapter.

Ideally, each place should be checked out IN PERSON by one or more members of your group before a choice is made. Because of busy schedules, this is rarely done or is done only by phone. Unless you are intimately familiar with the facility, this can lead to big problems, mostly having to do with facility size—the two factors being group size and live music. Whatever type of facility you choose, be sure it's large enough to hold your group comfortably. Don't forget to include spouses, teachers, and children in your count, if they are invited. An overcrowded situation will put a real damper on things.

Some places have a closing time of 2 a.m. Others close at 1 a.m. or midnight. We strongly recommend that you find a place that will allow you to be there until at least 2 a.m. Even this is not long enough for some people, but such folks can find an all-night restaurant or have a small party in their hotel or motel rooms.

But most important: How will you handle the problem of loud music versus conversation? **Live music ALWAYS requires a separate room where people can sit and talk without having to shout.** Any band is too loud for one room. (Disk jockeys are becoming more popular at reunions because with them the solution is simple: turn down the volume.) Check out the facility in person to make sure there is a second room, or the equivalent, where people can sit and talk. An adjoining bar will do if it's big enough and far enough from the band. And don't be fooled by the manager who tells you: "We have a reunion here every weekend during the summer, and we've never had any complaints." Some managers have very convenient memories when it comes to complaints, and their facility may be hosting an unending string of mediocre reunions. Your reunion should be "great," not "mediocre."

We should mention here a few things about food at reunions. Of course, as organizers, you should want the very best, or at least your money's worth. And of course, when you talk with banquet facility managers or caterers, they will always assure you that you will be getting a very high quality meal, that their chefs are very highly trained, that they have had much experience with reunions, have many satisfied customers, and then they will offer you a choice of several mouth-watering sounding menus with French sounding names which means it must be good. Don't be fooled. Reunions are notorious for having terrible food, the most common entree being roast beef that bears an uncanny resemblance to cardboard.

But the funny thing is, nobody seems to care. The memory of that terrible meal lasts a day or two (if that) and is forgotten. People go to reunions with other things in mind, and food is far down on the list of important items. Of course, you, as reunion organizers, will worry yourselves about it anyway because that is your job and as it should be. We are just here to tell you that, in the long run, it's not that big a deal.

After assessing your own situation (and reading the above), if you are still convinced that, for you, it IS a big deal, then we urge you to look very carefully into the meal-providing services of the facilities you have in mind. Keep in mind that the main reason for the lack in food quality is the whole process of catering. It takes a highly talented catering service to be able to prepare a fancy meal for several hundred people, transport it across town, serve everything at its own proper temperature, and have it all come out just right. What is usually served is nothing more than a re-heated meal. If your chosen facility has a full-time kitchen, then the quality may be a little better, but serving quality food to a large number of people is no easy task any way you look at it. It takes a lot of experience and know-how. But "the proof is in the pudding," as they say. If food quality is very important to you, then you have no alternative but to ask to sample the kitchen's (or caterer's) output in a real situation—like at a convention or another reunion. Offer to eat in the kitchen and to pay for the food.

Some facilities can be reserved without making a deposit until a few months before the reunion. Some will allow you to reserve two or more dates as long as you cancel all but one by an agreed upon deadline (though this is not common). Most have minimums (money and/or number of people) or guarantees that must be met. Each facility has its own rules in this regard.

We suggest looking now at: "The Facility" in Chapter 9.

Banquet halls and similar facilities can be found in the Yellow Pages under "Banquet Rooms." Country clubs are under "Golf Courses, Private" or "Clubs." For community centers try: "Playgrounds and Parks," "Recreation Centers," or "Social Service Organizations."

When to Have It?

Most class reunions are held from June through September for several good reasons: the weather is better; travel is easier; the kids are out of school; and summer is the traditional time for vacations. The next most common time is May followed by October. These gatherings tend to be well attended by the locals, but it can be inconvenient for those who live farther away. If you are getting a late start, you should hold your reunion later in the summer so that those who must travel have time to make plans. Of course, the earlier you notify everyone, the better your turn-out will be.

Don't plan a reunion during the year-end holidays. Even though many people will be in the hometown for the holidays, there is too much competition from other activities to have a well-attended event. The one exception to this rule is for school groups one to three years past graduation. For these folks it's just another year-end party and it can work. For almost any other group the nostalgic emotion involved in a reunion combined with the already high-energy and emotional year-end holiday can lead to a sense of "overload." Many people will simply be too emotionally drained to attend.

Reunions don't tend to happen during Memorial Day and Labor Day weekends because the school year is either just ending or beginning, which makes for a bad time for families to travel. Of course, with older reunions this may not make a difference. However, one difference it WILL make (and the same with the Fourth of July) is that travel and housing arrangements are more difficult during these holidays, not to mention the problems involved with renting a facility. The only thing in favor of three-day holidays is that they can better accommodate multi-day reunions.

Saturday is the most popular day for "single event" reunions. However, Sundays are good for picnics, barbeques, outdoor pot-lucks, and reunions of church affiliated schools (if the reunion is held at the school). In the latter case, a religious service is usually offered as an option in the reunion schedule.

How Much Should You Spend? (also see Chapter 5)

Last but not least, consider what you want to spend, which, of course, eventually translates into the cost per person. The total cost per person can range from almost nothing to $50 and more, depending on your ingenuity, donations, available labor, and what you are willing to do without.

Are any down payments or deposits required? Do you have the money for this? You may have to finance these initial expenses by borrowing from members of the committee or by having committee members pay their share ahead of time.

* * * * *

A LIST OF QUESTIONS TO ASK WHEN TALKING WITH THE MANAGER OF A FACILITY:

(These are just to give you a general idea as to the types of questions and the areas of questioning. Your own particular situation will dictate modifications, and/or additional questions.)

The manager will want to know how many people you expect at your reunion. Be prepared to give an answer (for help, see p. 30). However, an experienced manager can usually figure it out from the size of your graduating class, the year of graduation, and the last time you held a reunion.

(Fill in your own options within the parentheses.)

- What (Saturday nights) do you have open during (the first part of August)? How about (Sundays)?

- How do you charge? By the person or by the meal? What are the minimums? What must we guarantee? What about people who come late and don't eat? What about people who show up unannounced?

- How much of a deposit is required? By when is it needed? Is it refundable entirely or in part? What are the refunding rules? Is the deposit for "cancellation" only, or does it also include "breakage and damage"?

- How many people can you accommodate? Do you have different rooms to choose from? Can we rent a separate room away from the music? Is there a separate bar that is away from the music?

- Can you send us a floor plan of the room?

- Is a contract signed? What is in the contract that we should know about? Please send me a sample of your contract.

- When is closing time? How early can we start? When does the bar open?

- Who cleans up? When? That night or the next day?

- Can we decorate? What time can we start? What are the limitations? Can we use masking tape or thumb tacks? Who removes the decorations?

- Do you have your own kitchen? Is it operating everyday or only on the weekends? Do you have your own caterer? Can we have our own caterer? Can we choose what time we eat? Are there menu options? Can we have a buffet instead? What is the price difference? Are refreshments extra? Can we bring in our own refreshments?

- Can we come to a function to see your facility in action? Can we sample the food? (Offer to be discreet and to pay for the food.)

- Have you had other reunions from our school (from other schools in this area)? Can we contact some people in charge of these reunions? Can you supply names or phone numbers?

- Can we bring in our own wine for a toast during dinner? Are wine glasses available? (Don't forget the corkscrew.)

- Do you have a public address system? Do you set it up or do we? Do you have a stage or podium for the master of ceremonies?

- Do you have a slide (movie) projector and screen? Do you have extra bulbs? Extention cords? Table for projector? Duct tape to tape extension cords to the floor?

- Can you recommend a local band or DJ who plays our kind of music? Can you recommend someone who does balloon or flower displays or centerpieces? Can you recommend a photographer? A video company?

- Do you have extra tables and chairs for registration and displays of memorabilia? Do you have bulletin boards for memorabilia? Are they moveable? Do you have a moveable chalk board (for announcements)? Is there a charge for any of these?

- Do you have a coat and hat room? Is someone in charge of it? Is there a place for raincoats and umbrellas?

- What is the "smoking, non-smoking" policy? Do you have wheelchair access?

- Do you have ample parking? Is there a public lot nearby? Is there handicapped parking?

CHAPTER 3

Committees

*Getting Started – How Committees Work – Tips for Committee
Leaders – Did We Mention Fun! – Areas of Responsibility.*

Getting Started

The idea for a reunion usually begins with the nostalgia bug. You
start wondering whatever became of your senior prom date, or the
person with the locker next to yours, and eventually, wondering
gives way to longing to know. Pretty soon you are on the phone
trying to find out who is organizing the next reunion. You find that
no one is doing it, you take on the job, and that is how reunions are
born.

How they grow is another matter. The initiator (the person with
the original idea) is going to have to decide whether to continue
alone, with a few close friends, or open it up to a committee. One
person with prodigious amounts of time, energy and interest could
take on the whole project, but we don't recommend it unless it's a
very small reunion. Most reunions need a team effort; in other
words, a committee to share the work.

Contrary to popular belief, reunion organizers do NOT have to be
the class officers, or from the most popular clique, or those who
have become successful or well-known over the years. Nor do they
have to be the people who were assigned the job back in high
school, such as the class secretary or class historian. In fact, they
don't even have to be the people who organized the last reunion,
though, of course, it would be best to consult those people to see if
they have current intentions. Usually the committee is composed
of people who have stayed fairly close to home and, as a result, have
kept somewhat in touch with other local class members. They tend
to be genuinely interested in people and have a natural tendency to

help others. And, in general, they are people who are above average in organizational skills. As Ralph Keyes says in his book, *Is There Life After High School?*, (Little, Brown and Co., 1976), " ... I would advise personnel managers to hire a successful reunion organizer for any job in the outfit." Needless to say they should be people with enough time and energy to add the task of organizing a reunion to their regular schedule.

Normally it doesn't take more than a few days and a few phone calls to find out who is interested in working on the committee. The person who makes the first contacts is generally considered the leader, but at the first meeting he or she can accept or reject the leadership role. Perhaps that person is only interested in being the initiator, and doesn't want the responsibility of leading the committee. (If this is so, it's important that it be made clear right from the start.) If you don't have an obvious leader at first, one will probably appear, but occasionally 2 or 3 people become co-leaders, sometimes without even being officially designated. Regardless of how the leadership of your committee evolves, the main role of the leader(s) remains the same: to see that all the little details get done. Toward this end, one leader is usually more efficient.

How Committees Work

Even with large committees the actual organizing work is usually done by 2 to 4 people who work well together. So if your committee seems too large and people are still asking to join, this may not be as big a problem as it might seem. A large committee can be thought of as an advisory council. A lot of ideas will be tossed around at the meetings, and one function of the committee is to discuss and choose the ideas that it thinks will work best for the group. But when all is said and done, a handful of people will still do most of the work.

If this is not the first reunion for your class, and you didn't help with the last one, try to contact someone on the last committee. Perhaps they can provide advice, mailing lists, and (with luck) old bank accounts. You might consider including some of the previous organizers on the new committee. Occasionally (and this happens more than you might think) a new committee will form comprised of people who didn't like the way the last reunion was run. Still, it may not be necessary to make anyone feel excluded, even if they were on a committee which produced a reunion you didn't enjoy. Be diplomatic. After all, they will be invited to the reunion, too. Try to introduce new ideas without criticizing others.

If you have specific ideas about how the reunion should be run, you should be willing to sell them to the group. This may involve a fair amount of persuasive ability. Of course, you should also be willing to listen to the ideas of others. In addition, if you have an idea, you must be willing to be responsible for it. It's like being a parent. It's not enough to simply give birth to a great idea; you must be willing to tend it and stick with it until it's actually accomplished. If you feel strongly about your ideas, do your homework. Be prepared to show why an idea will work and invite others who support your ideas to attend the first meeting.

On the other hand, most truly great and innovative ideas can only be accomplished by an individual. Usually committees must compromise, which can really take the "genius" out of an idea. If you are committed to an idea and you can't get others to see your point of view, perhaps you should offer to do your project by yourself or with the help of a few people of your own choosing. This approach could work well if your project covers a particular part of the reunion (for example: decorations, a newsletter, a portion of the program, etc.), and if it doesn't cost too much or if you can figure out how to cover the cost.

Occasionally someone at the first committee meeting will find themselves face-to-face with their high school arch enemy, the person who stole their boyfriend/girlfriend, or maybe it's just someone whose attitude you never did like back in school. But people can change a lot over the years. The person you disliked back in high school is a different person today; so are you. You may find yourself working with (and actually liking) people you didn't care for years ago.

Tips for Committee Leaders

Suppose you are the committee chairperson. Volunteers have been found, sub-committees organized, jobs and authority have been delegated, things are getting done. If only it were that easy. Actually, this is where your job BEGINS. Once assignments have been agreed upon, YOU must follow up. Make sure the allotted duties are being done properly and within the assigned time period. You can accomplish this mainly by phone. Whatever you do, don't neglect it or just expect that people will maintain the same level of enthusiasm and commitment over the many months it takes to produce a successful reunion. You must provide leadership — and that includes motivation when the going gets tedious.

Make sure people are doing what they said they would do, and within the time-frame agreed upon. In the initial flush of nostalgia and excitement (and in a meeting with their former classmates looking on), people often take on more than they can handle. They have a hard time saying no. Several weeks down the line they may find themselves with a crucial job they have no time to accomplish. But someone has to do it. If you are keeping track of your volunteers, you can catch the over-committed ones before it's too late and assign some of their work to other people. However, be wary of taking on their tasks yourself unless you can see that it is absolutely necessary. You want to make it to the reunion without becoming a terminal stress case. You can't do everything. The idea is for you to delegate jobs and keep track so that everybody does their part and everything gets done. See the end of this chapter for a list of the various jobs.

It's also important that the proper people understand why, when, and how each task is being accomplished. For instance, if you understand the reasons behind our suggested name tags (see p. 110) or separate area for talking (see p. 12), but no one else does, you may not end up with the right results. Concepts are sometimes hard to get across. So ask questions, listen carefully to feedback, explain the overall plan again, and give concrete examples. Then, if necessary, repeat this process. This is time well spent. Understanding and accomplishment go hand in hand.

Did We Mention Fun?

In the welter of details and decisions it's easy to forget that reunions are supposed to be fun, even, or especially, for reunion organizers. After all, each detail and decision helps people come together, reconnect, and learn whatever they have to learn from the experience. Reunion organizers simply get a jump on the learning process. For them the reunion lasts months rather than just an evening. And while we have emphasized all the work involved, much of the planning, phoning, meeting and mailing is (or can be) fun in itself. Try not to lose sight of this when you are up to your elbows in mailing labels, or you think that you might have not charged enough per person and you are wondering where the extra money is going to come from. Jokes and laughter are the best ways to relieve tension and maintain friendships. So keep your sense of humor tuned and ready to roll.

Also, when the going gets rough remember to give yourself a pat on the back. At the beginning of this book we mentioned how important it is for people to re-evaluate the past, or at least share information with people they have known before. Your efforts will make this possible. Reunion organizers are catalysts. You are helping to create a time and place for people to reunite.

AREAS OF RESPONSIBILITY:
Here is a list of the various responsibilities that can be delegated. They can be assigned to individuals or sub-committees. Some can be combined. Some may not pertain to your situation.

1. Locating classmates.

2. Locating teachers.

3. Maintaining the filing system.

4. Budget/finances/bank account.

5. Bookkeeping.

6. Fund-raising.

7. Printed material: mailers, newsletters, surveys, registration forms, printed programs, etc.:
   a. Writing.
   b. Designing.
   c. Paste-up (in some cases).
   d. Photocopying/printing.

8. Mailing: addressing envelopes, folding, stuffing, stamping, sealing.

9. Information: Have someone available (by mail and phone) for classmates who have questions, information on missing classmates, donations, etc.

10. Food/beverage: Depending on the type of reunion, this could

cover pot-luck coordination, BBQ, snack tables, drink tickets, making arrangements with the caterer, supplying your own bar, one-day liquor license, etc.

11. Publicity: newspaper articles, ads, radio and TV announcements, use of marquees, banners across highways, notices on bulletin boards, etc.

12. Music: band/DJ/tape player.

13. Program: Master of Ceremonies, acknowledgements and thank you's, school song/sing-along songs, reading of letters from classmates or teachers who could not attend, jokes about school days, reading of class statistics, presenting awards/prizes, introduction of guests, benediction, toast, etc.

14. Extra events: picnic, BBQ, tours, church service, open house, sports event, etc.

15. Public address system.

16. Decorations: room, table.

17. Photography: group, individual, candid.

18. Memory book.

19. Video.

20. Registration (by mail).

21. Registration desk (at the reunion).

22. Host/hostess or welcoming committee.

23. Historian (keeper of the address list, scrap books, old movies, videos, mementos, etc.).

24. Compiling statistics/surveys.

25. Set up/clean up.

26. Activity centers: old slides/movies/photos, memorabilia table, letters from those who could not attend, posting of class statistics, residence map, refreshment table, memorial display, etc.

27. Name tags.

28. Door prizes.

29. Housing/RV arrangements.

30. Parking.

31. Selection and presentation of gift or scholarship to school.

CHAPTER 4

Meetings

The Basics – The Preliminary Meeting – The First Two General Meetings – The Third (and Hopefully Final) General Meeting.

The Basics

Meetings (along with phone calls, mailings, and a lot of running around) are the main means by which your reunion will take shape. And there is no way around it: You will have to hold meetings. However, there is no law that says they must drag on or be boring. Here are a few basic tips:

● Nothing is more frustrating or drains group energy faster than a poorly organized meeting where very little gets accomplished. Brush up on your basic meeting-leading skills, or find someone who is familiar with the process. (Please note that the leader of the meeting does not necessarily have to be in charge of the reunion. However, if this is the case, make it known from the start.)

● The most common place to meet is in people's homes. In the evening after dinner is usually the best time, but some groups prefer the weekends during the afternoon. An office, if you can locate one, is a very efficient place to meet. Many offices have meeting rooms with good lighting, comfortable chairs, long tables, chalkboards, coffee pots, and so on, and they lack the distractions of home such as television and kids. Meeting rooms can also be found in churches, schools, and community centers.

● It's a good idea to have some sort of refreshment at each meeting. Of course, you can accept donations of cookies and snacks, but otherwise this expense should come out of the reunion budget.

- As you talk to people on the phone before a meeting, ask them for agenda items (topics to discuss at the meeting). Then, at the start of each meeting, ask for additional agenda items prior to discussion of the first item. It may help to assign a time limit for each item. Appoint a timekeeper to remind the group that there are only five minutes left before you must move on to the next topic. As each item is discussed, check it off.

- The first meeting is really a mini-reunion. People are excited to see each other, so expect lots of talking and visiting. Bring the group back on course if people digress too much, as they inevitably will. If you need an authoritative source, show them this book and read them this line: "OK, you guys, let's settle down or we'll never get anything done!"

- While we are on the subject of this book: If you will check the back cover, you will notice that it says we will help the purchaser get reimbursed. If someone in your group has brought this book to a meeting, please offer to reimburse him or her out of reunion funds. If the person has intended it as a gift, no harm done. Surely by now you have noticed that it's worth its price.

- At each meeting, assign someone to write down an "action list." This is a list of all activities and the people assigned to, or who volunteered for, each activity. This list is typed up and mailed out to each committee member within a day or two after the meeting. Each person receiving the list should have his or her name high-lighted or underlined wherever it appears (use colored ink).

- **Remember to bring a class yearbook to all meetings.** The yearbook is your most valuable resource. You will use it to start compiling your mailing list and as a source of photos for name tags. You can also use it to jog your memory on teachers to invite, past events, and nostalgia of all kinds.

- A word on delegating authority. As we mentioned earlier, it's very important to spread out the necessary tasks so no one person works too hard. Also, the more committee involvement and enthusiasm you can generate, the more your reunion is likely to be a success—both because it will be better organized and because excitement and interest have an uncanny way of spreading. However, the people who accept responsibility for making decisions on behalf of the committee must agree to keep in mind the needs and interests of the whole group. If personal preferences are allowed to dictate, you may be in for a punk rock band when you had planned on an evening of golden oldies.

• Set the date for your next meeting before you adjourn.

• You can probably limit the total number of general meetings to three (four at the most) if you use your time **and the telephone** effectively. Sub-committees can meet to accomplish specific chores, but the whole group needs to get together only a few times.

• PLEASE NOTE: The timing of the meetings is actually dictated by the timing of the mailers. The first two meetings should be held just before the first mailer is sent out. (It takes two meetings to gather and decide about the information that will be contained in the first mailer.) The third meeting takes place just before the second mailer goes out. For information on mailers, see Chapter 8.

The Preliminary Meeting

An early preliminary meeting may or may not take place before the first general meeting. Its sole purpose would be to nail down a facility before they all get away (reserving a date and place), and is usually held so far ahead of time that only a small group (or maybe even one or two people) are involved. Of course, if a date and place have not been secured by the time of the first general meeting, then this item becomes the first issue on the agenda of that meeting.

The First Two General Meetings

The first committee meetings for most reunions are held either in the Fall (usually October or November) or in January — the reunion itself taking place the following summer. Either way is okay (though there is something to be said for getting an early start), but there are two important things to remember:

1. Regardless of when the first meeting takes place, the facility (in some cases) must be secured 12–18 months ahead of time.

2. Give a full 6 months notice to your classmates. In other words, if your first meeting is in January, be ready to send out your first mailer right after your second meeting. Don't dilly-dally around. That first notice should go out no later than mid-February.

If you are starting in January, then your first two general meetings should take place about one — not more than two — weeks apart; the second meeting is actually a direct continuation of the first. Various options are discussed at the first meeting and people are assigned to do research and gather information. At the second meeting decisions are made based on this information. The results of these decisions are then printed in the first mailer which should be mailed as soon as possible after the second meeting. If you are starting earlier than January (or earlier than 6 months prior to the reunion), then your scheduling of the first two meetings and of the first mailer can be a little more relaxed.

These are the items that should form the main part of your agenda at the first meeting (they are all discussed at length in other parts of this book):

• Decide on the type of reunion, choose a facility, and select a date (if you haven't already done so in a preliminary meeting).

• Gather information to determine the cost per person.

• Find people (discuss methods and divide up the list).

• Start the mailing list.

If you haven't reserved a facility before the first general meeting, do some phone research prior to the meeting to find out what's available, when, and the costs. It will also help if someone can visit each facility. Having this information available at the first general meeting will help the group make a quicker decision and can save a lot of time. Chapter 2 tells you what you need to know in this regard.

At the end of the first meeting, agree when and where the next meeting will be. Try to make it as soon as possible, but allow time for research — 7–14 days is about right. (Remember: If you are starting in January then try to get your first mailer out as soon as possible.) Make sure people are clear about their assignments and will be able to complete them in time for the next meeting. Mail out the "action list" as soon as possible after the meeting, and **follow up with phone calls to make sure assignments are getting done.**

At the second meeting your main job is to make decisions based on all the information and ideas you have gathered. Here is an agenda list for the second meeting:

- Make as many decisions as possible from the information you have collected, especially "date, time, and location."
- Pare down the list of "missing people" as much as possible.
- Make sure the mailing list is being handled properly.
- Set a cost per person (approximate is okay for now).
- Schedule a "mailer meeting" to address, fold and stamp the mailers. This could be a sub-committee job.

It's not possible to make every last decision at the second meeting. What's important is to research the various costs intelligently, get a sense for the range of costs, include all the expenses, and come up with an approximate budget. Using this budget (more about budgets in Chapter 5), you can figure the approximate cost per person.

Keep in mind that the first mailer is primarily an announcement —a way to collect money, and generate interest in the reunion. It's all right to have an estimated cost per person as long as it's labeled such. For example: "The estimated cost per person will be $25, plus or minus $3," or "The estimated cost per person will be $22–28." Also mention that the exact cost will be announced in the second mailer.

Most loose ends left over from the second meeting can be taken care of by telephone rather than another meeting. Let's say, for instance, that you have found that bands cost from $200 to $500 a night and at the second meeting you decide to spend $300. The actual reviewing and hiring of the band can be done at a later date. One person or a sub-committee can be assigned to do this so that another meeting won't be necessary.

The Third (and Hopefully Final) General Meeting

Except for a few small get-togethers (to address mailers, for example), it should not be necessary to have another general meeting until 6 to 8 weeks before the reunion. The purpose of this final meeting is to gather information for the second mailer and to discuss last-minute plans such as name tags, decorations, registration, refreshments, the program, and so on. It can also be a shot in the arm and confidence builder for the committee — after all, the last general meeting was several months before. This meeting can get them excited all over again.

If you feel other meetings are necessary, schedule them. However, if you run your meetings efficiently, three major ones (four at the most) should be enough, along with **lots of phone calls.**

CHAPTER 5

Finances

The Budget–Figuring the Cost Per Person–Tickets and Reservations–Bank Accounts–Bookkeeping–Under or Over Budget–Fund-raisers–Using Your Resources–Ways to Save Money (or The Frugal Organizer)–Raising Money Before the Reunion.

The Budget

Try to find someone who has a good head for figures and money management to work on the budget. Making decisions about money, in particular making sure that the income is more than the outgo, is an important part of a successful reunion. Of course, every well-managed household has such a person, so you shouldn't have to go too far afield to find one.

It's best to have one person in charge of the budget who can authorize all expenditures, keep the checking account, and maybe even do the bookkeeping. Remember, however, that there are different abilities needed here. The person in charge of the budget must be able to calculate when it's all right to spend money and when it isn't — in other words, be a good money manager. The person in charge of the books must be able to keep accurate records. If you can find one person with both these abilities, great. If not, or if one person simply doesn't have the time to do both, then have one person responsible for the budget and another for keeping books. Of course, they should work together very closely.

For the very first expenditures (like the first mailing, or a deposit for the facility), the money usually comes from:

- money left over from a previous reunion.
- committee members paying their share early.
- a personal loan from an individual.

Figuring the Cost Per Person

What makes a reunion possible, from an economic point of view, is that the costs are shared. The amount that each person must pay is calculated from a wide assortment of information, some of which is guesswork. The formula for coming up with the cost per person is actually quite simple. Estimate how many people will be attending, then divide that number into an estimate of the reunion's total cost. But coming up with the figures to plug into that formula is not a simple process.

Here are two important tips:

- Be as thorough as possible. Anything you leave out or miscalculate will cause a discrepancy.

- Since no one is perfect, include a "fudge" factor of about ten percent to help offset your mistakes.

Calculating the number of people who will attend can be a challenge. First try to find out the attendance at the reunions of the classes just before yours at your own school and/or neighboring schools. Try to work with percentages here if you can. The rule of thumb is to use **the percentage of the number contacted** who came, not the percentage of the class. (The reason being that committees that try harder to contact people will obviously get more people to come.) Then you can apply that percentage to the actual number of people you are contacting to project how many will attend your reunion. Of course, if this is not your first reunion, the most helpful figure will be the percentage of those contacted who attended the previous reunion, but this will work only if there is a constant number of years between your reunions. In other words, approximately the same percentage of people will attend their reunion if it's held every five years, every ten years, etc. But the more often it's held, the less the percentage of people who will attend. If this is your first reunion, or if you haven't had a reunion in a long time (20 years or more), then you can expect a much larger turnout.

If this is your first reunion and you can find no other source of information, you might try the managers of the various banquet halls in your area. They may very well have some statistics for you or be able to put you in touch with committees of previous reunions.

It's hard to think of every single item in calculating the total cost of a reunion. Here is a list of basic items you can use as a guide. You will find most of these items discussed separately and at length elsewhere in this book:

- rental of the facility.
- price of the meal.
- wine with meal or after dinner drink (necessary for toasts)—if not included in the price of the meal.
- cost of music (live band, DJ, taped music).
- photography/memory book.
- video.
- publicity and advertisement.
- cost of the mailers (calculated from: number of mailings, how many pieces in each mailing, how much postage per piece, plus printing or copying costs, envelopes, rubber stamps, etc.).
- decorations (for the room and tables).
- before-dinner and after-dinner refreshments (food, beverages, and table ware).
- awards.
- door prizes.
- name tags.
- printed programs.
- fund-raiser (items to auction or raffle, tickets).
- mementos (personalized take-home gifts).
- long distance phone calls.
- rentals (movie or slide projectors, sound system, extra tables or chairs, podium, bulletin board, punch bowl, utensils, etc.).
- guests (those who are offered a discount or not charged).
- clean-up charges.
- gift or scholarship for the school.
- fund for next reunion.
- fund for committee after-reunion party.

Some of the above items may not pertain to your reunion, or you may think of others you want to add. In any case, once you add up the grand total and add ten percent for oversights, you will have an estimated total to plug into the "cost per person" formula.

Try to arrive at a lump sum to charge per person rather than offering a lot of options. For example, instead of charging $20 for the event itself, plus $5 for a group photo, plus $5 for a memento, lump it all together with no options and charge $30 for the whole thing. However, the extras should be offered separately to those who can't attend. The cost per couple is usually twice that of a single, unless for some reason you want to offer a discount for couples (the singles may not like this arrangement). The cost for teachers (plus spouse or guest) runs the whole range from $0 to full price. It may depend on how many teachers are involved. If it's an older reunion and only a few teachers are still alive, you may want to have them as honored guests and not charge them. (Also see "Invite the Teachers," p. 61.)

Here are some helpful statistics that we have gathered, based on national averages. In the larger cities, the costs will be more; in the smaller towns, the costs will be less:

- For a dinner/dance reunion with alcohol available (but paid for separately), photographer, live music or DJ, sit-down dinner, awards, and memento (usually a photo booklet) the average is $25–30 per person (1989). This is the most common type of reunion.

- For a catered buffet, taped music, group photo (no individual photos), awards, no memento (other than group photo) the average is $15–20 per person (1989).

- Businesses that will organize your reunion for you are starting to spring up in the larger metropolitan areas (see Chapter 15, "Commercial Reunion Organizers"). The cost per person for a reunion organized by one of these businesses is around $42–55, depending mostly on the size of the class. Most of them will not "do" reunions of classes with less than 200 graduates; for some the cutoff is 250 or more. The above price is for an "all out" reunion with live music (usually a DJ), at a fancy hotel, individual photos, memory book, decorations (usually balloon bouquets as table center pieces), and all the mailing and contacting of people done for you.

Tickets and Reservations

At some point you will be collecting money. It's good business practice to indicate (to both you and the person paying) that a financial transaction has taken place, and "tickets" is often the first thing that comes to mind. But tickets cost money to print or buy. Addressing and mailing envelopes for sending the tickets takes time, and you have to pay for the envelopes and postage.

An easier and more common method is to indicate on ALL correspondence: "NO TICKETS WILL BE SENT—RECEIPT OF YOUR CHECK WILL RESERVE YOUR TICKETS AT THE DOOR." At the reunion you should have a list of those who made reservations, or the file records, available at the registration desk. There are actually no tickets involved. The name tag serves the purpose. At the end of Chapter 8 is an example of a Registration Form which can be sent out with your mailer, to be returned with a check.

A "pay-at-the-door" policy can be an absolute disaster. We highly recommend that you stay away from such a system. You will probably have to give a meal count to the facility manager a few days before the reunion, and you will be held responsible for paying for those meals. Or if you are preparing the food yourself, you certainly don't want to over- or under-buy. If you rely on "promises" (people saying they will be there, but not paying in advance), in almost every case you will be sadly disappointed. Some people will show up unexpectedly, and others who promised to be there won't attend. Even some people who have paid in advance may back out at the last minute, but at least they will not be a financial burden to you if they have already paid. Besides, asking for money in advance will give you the necessary "seed money" to start your reunion off right. There are several methods that can be used:

1. If the first mailer comes out 5-6 months (or more) before the event, ask for a percentage of the total amount (anywhere from 20 to 50% is appropriate) or ask for a set amount (say $10) per person. Then ask for the remainder in your second mailer.

2. If the first mailer comes out 4 months or less before the reunion (not recommended), you might as well ask for the whole amount. This also goes for people who are "found" within this time range.

3. Some reunions have found it useful to offer a small discount

($3–5 per person) to those who pay the full amount before a certain date. This will definitely get the money coming in. **Be absolutely certain that you mention a deadline in all of your mailers.**

Don't give full refunds to those who paid but couldn't attend. Something should be retained in direct proportion to the inconvenience that was caused — a few dollars or a small percentage is appropriate. State the refunding rules in your mailers. See p. 136.

Bank Accounts

Setting up a reunion checking account is good business practice. It eliminates the problem of having your personal finances mixed with reunion finances. It's a legal and permanent record of your transactions, and anyone who might question your finances can see the results in black and white (and sometimes red). Instead of having checks made out to your name, they can be made out to: "Central High School Reunion," or "Class of '61 Reunion, Central High," "C.H.S. Reunion," or whatever name your bank suggests. Many banks have a policy of allowing free checking accounts for temporary events such as reunions, but you will need to ask the bank manager about this. Phone several banks to see what their policies are.

Many reunions have two signatures required to withdraw funds. The drawback here is that getting the other signature can sometimes be time consuming and awkward. What if the other person goes on summer vacation just when you must pay the printer? A more realisitic approach is to have two or three people able to make withdrawals with just one signature required.

When the reunion is over and you are sure all the checks have cleared, you can put any left over money into a savings account to accumulate interest until the next reunion. This is a good time to have two signatures required for withdrawal.

When dealing with banks, the sticky part comes with interest-bearing accounts (checking or savings). Technically, the federal government requires that someone be responsible for paying taxes on the earned interest. This means the bank may ask for a social security number, and the person with that number must treat the interest from the account as part of his or her personal income. Of course, some people may be reluctant to do this. With a checking account you can get around this problem by opening a non-interest-bearing account. With a savings account many banks will allow you to register the account as owned by a non-profit group (the reunion committee). Non-profit groups are not required to pay taxes on such interest. The banks are simply trying to stay on the good side of the federal auditors, and such a category will usually appease them as long as there is not a huge sum involved.

It's best to deal with banks where you or someone in your group is well known. If someone in your group works in a bank, so much the better. Keep in mind that a bank manager DOES have the authority to set up the accounts in the manner described above. If you find yourself dealing with a "new accounts" clerk who seems reluctant, then ask to speak with the manager. If that doesn't work, try another bank.

Bookkeeping

You should get the books set up before responses start coming in. The reunion account check book can be used to record the deposits, withdrawals, and the balance. But a separate itemized record should be kept of all deposits. In this record each deposited check should be recorded with its number, who it's from, and the date of deposit. This is very important because this is the only record of deposit that you will have at the reunion. This record can be kept as a separate list, or on the bottom of each person's file record (see Chapter 7).

Under or Over Budget

Excess money. Extra money can always be saved for the next reunion (along with its accumulated interest), or even returned to the members. Perhaps your group could buy a gift for the school, or donate to a scholarship fund. Too much money is a problem that is easy to deal with. Not enough money, on the other hand, offers the committee a tougher challenge.

Not enough money. Running over budget is a big pain, but it DOES happen, in fact much more often than you may think (so don't be too embarrassed—if you were a financial wizard you might not have time to be planning a reunion). But before we mention the cure, let's first state the preventative rule:

IT'S BETTER TO TAKE IN TOO MUCH MONEY THAN NOT ENOUGH.

In black and white this means if you charge enough per person and collect in advance you will have no problems.

Too often, members of the committee will feel personally responsible for a deficit, and will make up the difference out of their own pockets. Now, if such a donation is made willingly, that's one thing. But too often it's done grudgingly, not knowing of any other recourse. If this is the case then it's time to plan a little fund-raiser.

Fund-raisers (also see "Raising Money Before the Reunion," p. 41)

There is usually no way to know that you will be short funded until a day or two before the event. This is because the last minute reservations and the last minute bills won't be available for tabulation until then. In fact, in most cases the final amount of income will not be known until the event itself. If three couples show up unannounced (assuming your policy allows for such exceptions, and we suggest that it does), at $60 a couple that's $180, which can easily be the difference between being in the red or being in the black. The important point is:

GO TO THE REUNION KNOWING EXACTLY WHERE YOU STAND FINANCIALLY, AND, IF NECESSARY, READY TO CONDUCT A FUND-RAISER.

This type of fund-raiser, of course, has to be quick and relatively simple. There is no time for elaborate preparations. The easiest way is to have a raffle. Raffle off a good bottle of wine or some other item of value or interest. Announce this on a large, prominent sign and place it right at the entrance next to the registration table where it can't be missed. Be specific—say how much you need to raise and translate that into an amount per person. The sign could look like Figure 2.

Announce the raffle a couple of times during the evening over the PA system. At the same time, send two or three people out among the crowd to sell tickets (make sure you get change from a bank ahead of time). Then during the program add up the amount

A well-tended private bar can make a lot of money. However, not all local laws allow such an endeavor.

FIGURE 2. A sign like this will sell a lot more tickets.

collected to see if it's enough, or do a quick calculation based on the
numbered tickets. Have the drawing at the end of the program.
(Have someone draw who is not an immediate part of the reunion
such as a band member, a food-server, or the manager of the
facility.) If necessary, give another push to sell tickets right before
the drawing. It's easier to sell tickets at this time because you have
a seated, captive audience.

Rolls of numbered theater-type tickets can be bought at
stationery or office supply stores. Get the double roll. These have
two tickets side-by-side with the same number, one for the drawing
pot and the other for the purchaser to keep. Stay away from the type
of tickets that require the purchaser to fill in name, address, phone
number, etc. This is too time consuming to do at an exciting event
such as a reunion, and will discourage people from buying a long
string of tickets. For a very high quality wine (entitled "Reunion,"
from Inglenook Winery), see Appendix A, Wine for Toasts.

Here is a tip from Hayward High School, Hayward, CA, Classes of
'52–'55. They created a very nice centerpiece for each table and next
to each centerpiece was an envelope with eight numbers (each table
seated eight people). At one point during the program each person was
given the opportunity to exchange a number for a dollar bill. Then the
MC drew a number from a hat (one through eight being the only
numbers available), and the person at each table with that number
took home the centerpiece. Of course, the trick here is to create a
desirable centerpiece that is worth considerably less than $8. In Hay-
ward's case, they were just trying to break even, but they still made
some money. Their centerpiece consisted of a small bottle of wine and
two wine glasses on a mylar plastic "silver tray" decorated with con-
fetti and streamers (school colors). Other possibilities abound.

Another option is to get a one-day liquor license, a volunteer bar-
tender, a supply of alcohol, and run your own profit-making liquor
concession (bar) during the event. This, of course, depends on your
local laws and the rules of the facility. But if it's possible it can be very
lucrative. Since it's impossible to know exactly how much liquor to
buy ahead of time, the only realistic way of doing this is to make
arrangements with a liquor store to take back unopened bottles. If you
can't make such arrangements, a self-run liquor concession is not
worth doing (unless you know someone who owns a bar and will
provide the liquor for you, or buy what you don't use).

Using Your Resources

Be sure to think of every possible way to use donations and volunteers BEFORE you spend money. Tap the talents of the committee, the members of your group, friends and spouses of the members of your group, or any local person who may be interested in helping out. Do you know people who are printers, typists, graphic artists, bookkeepers, writers, photographers, caterers, or have other skills to donate? Perhaps people would be willing to donate supplies. Are there farmers or gardeners who can donate or sell food cheaply for picnics, buffets, or hors d'oeuvres? Local businesses will often donate food, wine, flowers or other items in exchange for mentioning them in your mailers or at the reunion. Put an "items needed" and "help wanted" list in every mailer.

Don't overlook older children and spouses as a source of volunteer labor for help with mailings, clean-up, decorating, candid photos, bartending, registration, etc. Assess the personal experience and contacts of each member of the committee — you may be amazed to find you have most of what you need right there. There are only a few jobs that really require special skills. Some of these are bookkeeping, bartending, finding people, writing or editing the mailers, and master of ceremonies, to name the most obvious. Most of the other jobs just need people with enough time and energy.

Ways to Save Money (or The Frugal Organizer)

One of the biggest complaints about reunions is that they cost too much. Given this fact, it's surprising how many expensive reunions of the "dinner/dance" variety there are. Even difficult economic times don't seem to put a damper on them. The result HAS to be that a lot of poorer people are unintentionally being excluded. **Since every person, regardless of economic status, should have the right to attend his or her own reunion, we must encourage you to be careful about making your reunion too expensive.** If in doubt about how elaborate (and therefore expensive) to make your reunion, opt for the simpler and less expensive. You will be excluding fewer people and serving your group better by doing so. This is a big reason against commercially organized reunions.

It helps to remember that all your thinking, planning, figuring, and spending of money is for one basic goal: that people have a good time and feel comfortable at the reunion. Some of those attending will have a good time and feel comfortable while spending a lot of money, and some won't. In many cases (especially public school reunions, which represent more of a cross-section of society) the elapsed time since graduation can be a factor. Younger people just starting out with families and careers tend to have less spending money than older people. Once you begin the budgeting process, and come up with some approximate figures, you will get a better sense of what you want to afford.

But let's say you have added it all up and it costs too much. This book focuses on one of the most expensive types of reunions — a dinner/dance in a banquet hall with a photographer, band, and so on. That's because a very large percentage of reunions are of this type. However, there are many fine reunions held each year that cost virtually nothing or, at least, a lot less.

There are lots of ways to cut back on expenses. Public or private parks, Grange Halls, school gyms, and community centers are either free or inexpensive, so you can cut the cost of facility rental substantially. Having a buffet instead of a sit-down dinner is a pleasant and less costly alternative (and gives people a better chance to mingle). Serving just hors d'oeuvres or snack foods is even cheaper. Pot lucks and BBQ's are fun and may serve your group quite well, but keep in mind that most out-of-towners can't be expected to bring more than what is easily available in a grocery store.

Where else can you cut back? Is a live band necessary? Are individual photos necessary? How about awards? Decorations? There are many possibilities to explore. It's up to you, but here is a general rule: To save a lot of money, it's best to cut back on one or two expensive items rather than lots of smaller inexpensive ones. Often the small items are necessary to make it a smooth running, enjoyable event.

If you feel that you absolutely MUST eliminate one major expense, we recommend that you do without "live" music (or a DJ, since they cost about the same), and instead have your own taped music or records. It's not that hard to be your own DJ. It won't be the class act of a professional, but it will be adequate. This will easily save you $200–500. The bottom-line basic "need" at a reunion is communication, not entertainment.

The single biggest demographic factor affecting the cost of reunions is "rural vs. urban." All other things being equal, a reunion held in a large metropolitan area can be $10–15 more per person than one held in a small town. Of course, the tastes of urban dwellers usually run a bit to the more expensive side (or at least, they are used to spending more money). But other than this, the main reason for the difference is the cost of the facility (which usually includes the dinner). If you live in a large city and want to save money, consider renting a community or social hall and having your own caterer. The large hotel chains and country clubs are always the most expensive way to go.

Raising Money Before the Reunion

Another option to consider is raising money in advance. Some groups have tried various income-generating schemes. We know of one class that holds a very successful all-alumni dance at their school every year and raises enough money to finance their reunion in style. How about an auction or flea market sale? Or raffle off two tickets to Hawaii (travel agents can help you here). Also, check to see what church, community, and service groups do for fund-raisers in your area.

Cookbooks are a big item with some family and military reunions, but a few private school and college reunion groups are also trying their hand at it. It usually takes the funding and persistance of a permanently organized group to create a cookbook — which leaves out most public school reunion groups. These books come spiral bound and are sold to members of the group as well as to friends, relatives, and the general community. Most of the printers who specialize in creating cookbooks for fund-raisers have "how-to" instructions available. See Appendix A for a list of printers, and information on a useful book entitled *How to Publish and Sell Your Cookbook*.

CHAPTER 6

Finding People

(Also see "Finding People" in Chapter 12, "Military Reunions.")

*The Scope of This Chapter – Using the Sherlocks in Your Group –
How Much to Budget? – At Your First Meeting – Using the
Telephone – Dealing with Directory Assistance – School Records –
Newspapers, Radio and TV – Other Methods – Make Your Mailers
Work for You – Include Everyone – Invite the Teachers – Sources
for Finding People.*

The Scope of This Chapter

People are always asking us for more advice on how to find
people, as if there were some magic formula that we accidently
forgot to include in this book. We are not going to pretend that we
have included everything here, but if there is an easy way, we
haven't found it yet. And even though computer technology is
making it harder for people to hide, it will be a few years until the
average person will be able to easily "access" the whereabouts of
another person from the convenience of their home computer. And
even then, the database will be something like a "national
phonebook": full of people who don't mind being found.

The truth is, it takes a lot of hard work and persistence to find
people. More than 99% of the information you are looking for is in
some computer or some file somewhere in the country. 100% of it
is in someone's memory somewhere. It's just a matter of how to get
to it. If you are diligent, have a lot of time, and it's very important to
you to find the information (such as the case with many people
doing family and military reunions), then the chances are good that
you will succeed. However, with school reunions there is usually

not enough time, money, or interest to exhaust all the options and resources that are available. In the back of this chapter are listed the sources that are the easiest and most productive to access, to be used after you have exhausted the "grapevine." For an amazingly thorough book on the subject, we recommend *You Can Find Anyone*, by Eugene Ferraro, available through us. See the coupon on p. 221, and a description in Appendix A.

Many people on reunion committees don't seem to completely understand the importance of trying to find their former classmates. A half-hearted job will result in a lot of people right under your nose who didn't get "found." And as you know, the grapevine is amazingly efficient. Once these people find out that no one really bothered to look for them, and they missed the reunion as a result, some of them will not think too highly of your organizing abilities and efforts. Also, apathy is contagious. You may have a hard time convincing people to help the next time around if you don't give your current reunion an all-out effort. The time and effort spent finding people will not only help your present cause, but it is also a wise investment in future reunions.

These are the general techniques discussed in this chapter:

- using the grapevine (asking questions by phone, in person, and through the mail).
- searching school records.
- announcements in local newspapers, on radio and TV.
- using your reunion mailers.
- searching public and private records.

Here is a brief outline of the steps you should take (in order):

1. At your first meeting, go through your Junior and Senior yearbooks, name by name. Everyone makes a list of the classmates they think they can find. Discuss some of the techniques in this chapter, and especially the information on using the telephone.

2. Send the missing person list out in your first mailer, and in it ask for volunteers who would enjoy the job of "finding people." Allow a few weeks for people to respond.

3. Go to your school with the missing person list. Get whatever information they will give you. Also, look into other information you can get at the school. (See p. 52.)

4. Give the missing person list to the best detective-types in your group. Call them occasionally with encouragement and ideas. Make sure they are trading information. Get them their own copy of this book. See order form in the back.

5. Send a REVISED missing person list out with each of your mailers.

6. From here on it gets harder and harder. Each "find" is cause for a minor celebration. Depending on the time, energy, and interest of your group, look into some of the sources listed in the back of this chapter.

Using the Sherlocks in Your Group

Many reunions do little more to find people than use the local telephone book and print the missing person list in their mailers. That's because to really dig for those "hard-to-finds," it takes someone with curiousity, a knack for detective work, and persistence in following leads. Some people hate to do this and some people love it. Try hard to find people in your group with these traits (advertise in all mailers). Such people may not even be interested in attending meetings or serving on the committee. But don't waste their time. Give them the missing person list AFTER you have made a reasonable effort to get it as small as possible.

You might try to enlist the help of any private investigators who may be in your group, or married to someone in your group. Their methods and contacts make them real pros in the business of "finding people." However, be sure they understand that you are asking for free help. Their hourly wage usually starts at $40 and goes up from there.

Others who may have access to records and files not ordinarily available to the public are people who work for: the police, FBI, state department of motor vehicles, the welfare or unemployment offices, credit unions, banks, social security, utility companies, and phone companies. However, in some of these cases it may not be exactly legal for these people to access their files for "reunion purposes." Of course, you are only looking for an address or phone

number, not their life history. But after your initial "suggestion,"
don't push your "contact" too hard. You don't want to get anyone
in trouble.

How Much to Budget?

This is going to depend a lot on how much interest in finding
people there is in your group. It always takes at least one, and
hopefully three or four, INTERESTED people to accomplish this job
properly. If you have such people, it is usually cost effective to aim a
little more money their way. If they find 20 extra people, say ten
show up, at $60 a couple that comes out to $600 that you wouldn't
have had otherwise.

A good rule is to budget at least $1 per classmate, and go up from
there when you find some Sherlocks in your group. Since the effort
of these people will probably at least pay for itself, it's an item that
can easily be added to the budget as you go along. Just be sure to
keep a close watch on it (especially the phone calls); there may
come a time when it will no longer be cost effective. Usually,
however, the interest in finding people runs out before the money.
By the way, the money budgeted for this purpose usually goes for
actual expenses such as telephone, postage, and search fees. You
might consider paying for gas and travel expenses, depending on
your particular situation. Labor costs (hourly wages) are almost
never covered; the job is considered voluntary.

At Your First Meeting

Although finding people can be hard work, the first stage can be a
lot of fun. Here is where your trip down memory lane really starts.
BUT there is no subject that will take your meetings off on more
tangents. You should begin this process at your first meeting, and it
helps to have a strong leader who can keep the discussion on track.
If you can't keep the meeting focused, you are likely to be there into
the wee hours reminiscing about old friends and classmates (fun,
but not too productive).

Have plenty of paper and pencils on hand and a batch of lined file
cards or binder paper, depending on your system. Turn to Chapter 7
and read about the various record-keeping systems.

Start by going through your Junior and Senior yearbooks—**be sure to have these yearbooks at every meeting.** Have one person read off the names while the others write their lists. Committee members should each make their own list of people they think they can find. At first, have each name appear on only one searcher's list (otherwise, the person may be bothered by too many "contacts"). Later, with the hard-to-finds, a name can be on anyone's list. Be sure that no one is forgotten or overlooked. At the same time all this is going on, have someone (maybe the person reading off the names) write down the names, one name per record. (This task can also be done ahead of time by some industrious soul.) Then at the bottom left of each record write the searcher's initials. (See Figure 7.) These records should be kept in order by last name, and will eventually find their way into different sub-files. For right now simply make three piles. The largest pile will be the "original" file (no addresses yet). The second will be the meager beginnings of your mailing file, and at your first meeting will contain only the cards of those whose addresses are easily obtained, like the committee members and maybe a few close friends. The third is the deceased file. (A teacher file could also be started if you are inviting the teachers.) The keeping and maintenance of these records is explained quite thoroughly in the next chapter, and by the flow chart on p. 67.

In order to get the missing person list ready for the first mailing (which comes out right after the second meeting), have your committee members concentrate their people-finding efforts during the time between the first two meetings. The grapevine should really get warmed up and buzzing. Encourage the committee members to involve others, not on the committee, in this process, too. You can't have too many people doing this job.

Using the Telephone

Word-of-mouth is the most common means of finding people, and the telephone is the most common tool used in this process. When talking to classmates (either in person or by phone), try to "draw out" the information that is inside of them. Most people don't realize that what they know can be useful in locating someone. A good question to start with is: "Who were your best friends?" After all, these are the people they will probably know the most about. Make a list of these people (the ones that are still missing) on the back of the informant's card or record. Then, as you are talking about a particular "missing" person, ask the questions on the following list:

(Give two copies of this list to all committee members and anyone who volunteers to help find classmates. Ask them to keep one copy by the phone and the other in their wallet or purse.)

– – – – – – – – – – – –

LIST OF QUESTIONS TO ASK REGARDING A MISSING PERSON:
(NOTE: When talking with a stranger, always mention that your purpose is for a reunion.)

1. Names of missing person's best friends.
2. Names (and years in school) of the person's brothers, sisters, or cousins.
3. Parents' names.
4. College or trade school attended.
5. Church attended.
6. Occupation(s).
7. Town moved to.
8. Married name (for women).
9. Wife's maiden name (for men).

And remember the first rule of finding someone: If you can't find the person directly, find someone who CAN find them.

– – – – – – – – – – – –

When looking through phone books, and when calling Directory Assistance, remember that the main objective is to get the address. The phone number is important, too, but your first attempt at contact should be through the mail. It will be cheaper to mail the information to the non-locals, and besides, you have to send them the mailers anyway. Use the telephone if the person doesn't respond to the mailing (it may be that the address was incorrect), or if the person was "found" just before the reunion.

When checking phone books, start with the areas nearest you. Your local library will have these phone books, but also check with your local phone company to find out which phone books they will send you free. Check:

1. under the full name of the classmate.

2. under the full name (which you got from the school records) of the parent or guardian.

3. under the last name (especially if it's an unusual or uncommon name) for possible relatives.

4. for a man, under his wife's maiden name (for possible in-laws).

These last two steps may be hopeless for a Smith or a Johnson, but could work quite well for a Kradowsky. Let's say, for example, that you notice a Kradowsky in the phone book, but the first name is wrong. You phone that particular Kradowsky and find out that the person you are looking for is his first cousin who moved to Podunkville, PA, ten years ago and they have been out of touch. Next, dial "00" (long distance operator) and ask for the area code of Podunkville, PA. Then dial the area code plus 555-1212 for information in Podunkville.

All public and college libraries have a large assortment of current phone books from the major metropolitan areas around the country (however, calling first could save you a lot of time). Libraries or sections of libraries that are specifically for genealogical research (tracing family history) have truly amazing collections of phone books and city directories that are both out-of-date and current. For example, The Sutro Library in San Francisco, which is by no means the largest, has on hand 15,000 city directories and 10,000 telephone books. City directories (also called criss-cross directories) are put out by private companies and contain two separate listings: alphabetical by name and by street address. The alphabetical list includes the person's occupation, but you will have to turn to the address listing to find the phone number. See p. 57 for more on how to use city directories. For genealogical society libraries in your area, look under "Libraries" in the Yellow Pages. Your state library system should be the best, or at least largest, source.

These days don't assume that just because a woman is married, that it's hopeless to look under her maiden name. Many women are retaining their maiden names, and appear under separate listings in the phone book. If you know her husband's last name, you might also try looking under a hyphenated version of their combined names. Of course, if you are involved with a 50 year reunion, these rules would probably not apply.

You should make it easy for classmates to communicate with the committee. One way is to include a phone number (two, if possible) in all your mailers. Some people are very impulsive and "phone oriented." They will make a call, but won't bother to write. Give out the phone numbers of people who:

1. are willing and able to field phone calls.

2. are reasonably gregarious and enthusiastic.

3. are near the phone much of the time, especially in the evening.

4. have a phone answering machine.

A big advantage of using the telephone is that it's a personal approach. A real live voice on the other end of the line is a lot different than a notice in the mail, and can easily elicit the "nostalgic interest" necessary for the person to say: "yes, I want to be there!" We suggest phoning all the "non-responses" 6 to 8 weeks before the reunion (right after the second mailer is a good time). Don't be pushy, but just mention that you would really like to see them again, and that everyone is in the same boat about being a little nervous about the whole prospect of a reunion, even the reunion organizers. If at all possible, have someone make the call who "best knows" the person being called. Using the phone in this way will definitely turn out to be cost effective. If you talk only five extra people into attending, at $60 a couple that's $300. And at the very least, you get to verify some addresses in your "unverified" address file.

Since most people must use their own phones, they may shy away from a volunteer job that costs them money. These days even dialing Directory Assistance costs money. It's necessary to budget for telephone calls as part of the reunion expense, and to let volunteers know they can be reimbursed. It's also a good idea to put a limit on the cost (or time) of each long distance call since some people find it awkward to cut short a conversation with someone they haven't talked to in a long time. A set limit will give them an excuse to keep the conversation brief. You might also have a rule that if they go over the time limit, that they must pay for the additional charges. Of course, all this requires they keep a list of the phone calls they make.

Let's say you find a name you are looking for in a phone·book. Even the middle name or initial is the same, and you are reasonably sure the person is (or was) somewhere in the area. You phone the number and are informed that the number is disconnected or no longer in service. Don't give up! Call Directory Assistance to see if another number is listed. The number may have been published wrong. The person may have recently moved and the phone company messed up in referring the number. If that doesn't work, send a post card to the address in the phone book (if one is listed). If the person moved, the Post Office is likely to forward mail longer than the phone company is likely to refer the phone number. Or the person presently at the address may forward the post card. Or a letter written to the person presently at the address (addressed to: "Resident") may net you some information—if only the city that the person moved to. Persistence is the name of this game.

The cheapest times to call long distance are usually from 11 p.m. to 8 a.m., all day Saturday, and Sunday until 5 p.m. (your time). But it depends on the rules of your long distance carrier.

If anyone in your group has access to an outgoing WATS line, you might see if it can be used in the evenings or on weekends.

Some interesting facts about unlisted phone numbers:

● One third of all residential phone numbers are unlisted, and the more affluent a person, the more likely the number is unlisted.

● Sometimes an unlisted number will appear in a city directory.

● Directory Assistance in some areas (it depends on the rules of the local phone company) will tell you if the name you are looking for has an unpublished (unlisted) number. You won't get the number, but at least you will know that the person (or a person with that name) is in the area. This convenience is slowly being phased out all over the country.

Dealing with Directory Assistance. Information operators have an infuriating tendency to behave very much like the equipment they are using: computers. Unfortunately they are not very good at it.

Most of them are talking to each other between calls (and, therefore, not giving their full attention to you). And in addition they must average a certain number of calls per hour, so they are not too anxious to "linger" while you collect your thoughts when the name you ask for doesn't immediately turn up.

Our estimation, made over a period of about five years, is that Directory Assistance is wrong or misleading about 10% of the time. Sometimes they give you the wrong number (if you report this, by the way, you will get credit for the call—no questions asked). Other times the name is there, they just can't find it. Or more precisely, they don't want to bother checking various spellings or initials, so they just look under the exact name you ask for and if it's not there, you lose. There is no way for you to know if they are checking other options or not. So you have to be explicit. If you ask (for example) for the number of a David Charles MacKenzie, and are informed that it's not there, then ask for "initials D.C.," "initial D.," "D. Charles," and MacKenzie spelled with "Mc" instead of "Mac." The lesson here is that if you are VERY interested in finding a person, then you should try Directory Assistance more than once.

You are usually allowed three "look-ups" (sometimes two — depends on the area) per phone call to Directory Assistance, but you have to let the operator know right away that you are looking for more than one number. Then you will get the first number(s) by real live human voice and the last by that infernal electronic voice called an audio response unit. One trick that can be used in order to get a human response and/or to keep the operator on the line for other questions, is to tell the operator that you are looking for more than one number.

Many people don't realize that in most areas it is possible (and legitimate) to get an address from the Directory Assistance Operator, which could ultimately save you a phone call. You must ask for the address right from the start. You will then get the address (or be informed that there is no address listed) from a real live operator before being turned over to the electronic voice for the phone number.

School Records

All schools must legally keep a scholastic record of anyone who ever attended the school. These records also happen to contain the address of the parent or legal guardian, as well as the full name and birthdate of the student. But each state has its own rules about whether this is public information or not. In most states the person's scholastic record is confidential, but the address and birthdate are not. Also, many rural and smaller schools make exceptions if the information is for reunion purposes. Contact the school secretary or Activities Director at your school and let him or her know that your class is planning a reunion. Provide the name, address and phone number of your committee contact, so that inquiries to the school will be referred to your reunion committee. Ask if you can look through the school records. In most cases they would prefer that a school employee look up the information for you. To not waste anyone's time, it's best to have the missing person list as small as possible. If your school no longer exists, call the school district office to find where the records have been stored. Unless they have been destroyed by fire or flood, they are someplace. They can't legally be thrown away.

From the school records, you should copy (or request):

1. full name
2. last known address   } for sure
3. birthdate
4. parents' full names
5. parents' occupations   } if available
6. social security number

While you are at the school, check the school library and yearbook office for other sources, such as:

1. Yearbooks 3 to 4 years prior to your senior year, and class photographs. These may yield names of people who dropped out or moved before graduation.

2. Graduation programs or official lists of graduates. May yield names of people who moved to the area near the end of their senior year and were too late to appear in the yearbook. (Also, local papers usually print a list of graduates.)

3. Yearbooks of other classes before and after yours. Checking 6 to 8 years before and after your class may yield names of brothers, sisters, or cousins of classmates. This works very well with unusual or uncommon names.

Also ask the school office for the phone numbers of reunion committees of classes plus or minus 6–8 years from yours. It is very worthwhile to have these committees check their files for brothers, sisters, or cousins—especially with an unusual last name.

Newspapers, Radio and TV

A good free source of publicity for your reunion, specifically geared to finding classmates, is a **press release** printed in your local newspaper(s). In general, small town papers, or community papers within large cities, will be more receptive to a release and may even print the entire missing person list. But larger papers may take your information also, provided you keep it short, neat, and to the point. Delegate this job to someone who has a typewriter and can turn out a professional looking release. It should be only a paragraph or two, double spaced, and get right to the point: name of school, year of graduation, date of reunion, and the fact that you are looking for people. Be sure to include a phone number. Also, the person who prepares the release should include his or her name and phone number so the paper has someone to contact if there are any questions. See Figure 3.

```
PRESS RELEASE
For release: Immediately
Contact: Mary Smith 415/555-5555

Lakeside High School Class of '49 Reunion

Lakeside High School of San Francisco, CA, Class of '49

will be having its 40th reunion on Saturday, August 19.

For more information call Bill Jones at 415/555-4444.
```

FIGURE 3. *"Press Release" is a newspaper term, and "Public Service Announcement" is a radio term, but in reality the exact same form can be sent to either. It's acceptable for the title "Press Release" to appear on the form sent to radio stations.*
From the example above, please note: 1. Always double space the text of a Press Release. 2. The exact time and place is not necessary since interested people must contact Bill Jones anyway. Keep it as simple as possible. 3. Mary Smith is the contact for the newspaper or radio station to call if they have any questions about the press release. Bill Jones is the name that will be printed or read over the air for members of the class to contact. These two contacts do not need to be the same.

NOTE: If there is ANY possibility that the missing person list can be printed in a newspaper or read over the air, then by all means take advantage of such a service. However, most newspapers and radio stations have a policy or format that must be followed in regards to "reunion announcements" that usually does not include such a list. Call first to find out.

These releases should be sent out from 3 to 6 months before the reunion, as it may be several weeks before the paper can find space to run them. The best way to insure your material will be used is to follow through with a phone call, or better yet, to make a personal contact at the paper. The people most likely to use your informa-

---

BAKER HIGH SCHOOL CLASS of '79 is planning a 5-year reunion to be held Nov. 24. The committee is asking for help in locating the following classmates and anyone knowing where they live now can call 236-8288:

Pamela L. and Pat Adams, Scott Akers, Debra Ball Anderson, Jeff Anderson, West Anderson, Doug Beebe, Linda Bowling, Debbie Bradford, Ray Cheatham, Richard Combs, Donna Dimski, Marian Cosner Dionne, Molly Eardly, Randy Eastham, Carroll Figueroa, Glen Hall, Fawzia Heeres, Scot Helton, Robin Hood, John Humphries, Robyne Jones, Tina Kennedy, Ron Kregh, Keith Ingram, Mike Leggitt, Marcella Lejk, Scot Lewis, Brenda Lowry, Gail Malone, Marie Coates Marks, Greg McPheters, Dale Milby, Donna Jean Moore, Tim Morrison, Bill Moss, Holly Mote, Sandra Penix, Katrina Pennell, Doug Risk, Janet Roberson, John Shirley, Eric Stinson, Wendi Stanton, William Stanton, Lynne Thomas, David Todd and Terri Pottenger.

Class of '74 reunites

The reunion committee for Hutchinson High School graduating class of 1974 has planned its reunion for June 22-24.

The following class members have not yet been located: Kathleen Amick, Tony Aubert, Shirley Ayste, Jennifer Brandt, Jim Brown, Bill Caldwell, Roxane Cochran, Jon Davis, Peggy Edwards, Tim Erickson, Joel Hill, Tom Maulder, Cindy Flores, Barbara Gabehart, Denise Gliddenn, Dana Hall, Deean Hall.

**JOIN BALBOA ALUMNI
CALL FRANK SMITH
(415) 555-1234**

Class of 1944 sets reunion

The Colorado Springs High School Class of 1944 will hold its 40th year reunion July 27-29.

Anyone with information on classmates' whereabouts are asked to call Vern Collier, 473-3230 or 632-8358, or write Box 112, Colorado Springs 80901.

Members of the classes of 1943 and 1945 are also invited.

FIGURE 4. *Use your local newspaper. However, most papers will not print the "missing" person list.*

tion will be someone in charge of a "coming events" column, or the society page editor. Some papers even have a special section for reunions. Please remember that newspapers are high-pressure places — if you call right before a deadline you may get a curt response. Most reporters will be happy to talk to you after the deadline has passed.

We don't recommend ads in the "personals" or "announcements" section of the want ads. You don't get enough response for your money. An exception, of course, would be if you had an "in" with the newspaper and access to free advertising.

If your press release is brief and cut to a bare-bones minimum (as the example in Figure 3), it can double as a public service announcement (PSA) for the local radio stations. (It's even okay to keep the title of "press release.") Of course, if you have an "in" at the radio station, then you can try for a wordier PSA, but as a rule radio stations are even more succinct than newspapers. A radio station either has a policy of reading reunion announcements or it doesn't, and you are wasting your time sending PSA's to one that doesn't. Every large city has at least one or two stations that will oblige. Call first to find out. The best way to get the phone numbers (and addresses) of radio stations is in the Yellow Pages under "Radio Stations," otherwise in the very front of the "K's" in the white pages.

The only TV stations that will carry reunion announcements are the small local cable stations. Look under "Television Stations" in the Yellow Pages.

Other Methods

Some ambitious organizers have used overhead banners across main thoroughfares in their communities to announce their reunion. Of course, this requires someone in your group who can make a banner. The cost of having it made professionally would probably be prohibitive. Your local utility company or city maintenance crew is usually in charge of putting it up. Also, you may have to sign up on a waiting list. Ask city hall or your Chamber of Commerce for details.

Make use of the marquees in your hometown. Most of these are used for advertisement purposes and, therefore, are of value to the owner or proprietor. So just ask to use it for two or three days at the most. Your local school marquees may be available for a week or more, especially during Christmas or Easter break and during the summer.

If someone in your group has the time and inclination, he or she could go to an old address and ask the neighbors if they have any information on the people being sought. Just the name of the town they moved to could be of help (see list of questions to ask, p. 48). This method usually works if the family lived in the neighborhood for a long time.

Another way of searching the neighborhood is by phone, but you will have to go to a library and look through the city directories to do this. These city directories are arranged in alphabetical order by street address, as well as by name. With the help of a street map, you should be able to find the phone numbers of most of the people living in the area. Then if you compare the old city directories with the new, you can figure out who is still living in the neighborhood.

FIGURE 5. *A banner across the main street in town will get attention.*

When you make these phone calls, remember to always mention that it is for a reunion. Also, leave your name and phone number with them in case they remember something later.

Don't overlook notices in your local church, business, swapper, or school newspapers or newsletters. These usually accept reunion announcements at no charge. Notices can be posted on bulletin boards in local laundromats and grocery stores. Some bulletin boards will accept only 3 × 5 card size or smaller, and notices usually must be dated.

Members of ethnic or close-knit religious groups are very likely to be in touch with each other, at least through the grapevine. You might want to check with a church or synagogue which some of your classmates may have attended, or contact ethnic or community organizations, especially those offering memberships and newsletters. Perhaps membership lists can be checked or announcements printed in newsletters.

School reunion organizers are always complaining that it's so difficult to find someone who has joined the military. If the person is still on active duty, this is simply not true. You just have to know who and how to ask, and the branch of service that the person is in. (It also costs $3.50 per search unless you know someone on active duty who can make the inquiry for you.) If the person is retired from the military or in the Reserves it can be a little more difficult, but still quite possible. See Chapter 12, "Military Reunions" for details.

Make Your Mailers Work for You

Be sure to include the missing person list in EVERY mailer you send out. (Mailers are covered thoroughly in Chapter 8.) In addition, make a plea for help in locating classmates. It's easy for people to forget about this or put it off until later, assuming that someone else will do it. Mention in the mailer that the reader may very well be the only one who knows the whereabouts of a particular individual. Explain that it's important to try to locate and include everyone in the reunion. Emphasize that even a small clue can help. You might want to write something like this at the bottom of the missing person list:

If you don't have their address, send us a clue:

   —names of their best friends in school.
   —someone who now knows them.
   —the college they attended.
   —a company they worked for.
   —where they moved to.
   —parents' names or whereabouts.
   —names (and class) of brothers, sisters, or cousins
   who also attended the school.

We'll do the investigating. Every small clue helps.
Thanks for your help.

This type of assistance is so important that some reunions announce a prize to be given at the reunion for "Best Detective" (or The Sherlock Holmes Award). A cash prize (for every "found" person who attends the reunion) is also appropriate since, if done properly, it can be cost effective.

When asking a complete stranger for someone's whereabouts (whether on the phone or in person), ALWAYS mention that it's for a reunion. It's surprising how many people will try to "cover up" for someone else, even if they don't know the person.

The missing person list will become shorter as responses come in from classmates and as a result of your other efforts. For the stubborn cases, you might refer to the "parent or guardian" address copied from the school record. Send a short note to that name and address, requesting information (be sure to mention that it's for a reunion). Of course, with older reunions this may not be appropriate since the parent or guardian may be deceased.

If this isn't your group's first reunion, try to get the old mailing list. However, use it mainly to provide clues for locating people, or in case you absolutely can't find current information on a person's whereabouts. Old addresses are often wrong. The purpose of getting the old list is just to give you something to work from. But if you can't get an address in any other way, send an announcement to the old address. Remember: if you don't receive it back by mail, don't necessarily assume that the addressee received it. The person now living at that address (if it slipped past the Post Office's mail forwarding system — which is quite possible) may have thrown it away. Also, "mail forwarding" is good for only one year at the most, and in metropolitan areas, 6 months. You might consider putting the words "Please Forward!" on the outside of your mailers (but see next paragraph first). You might also consider writing a letter to the "occupant" or "current resident" of the address to see if they might know the whereabouts of the person you are looking for. They might not know the exact address, but they may know (for example) the city to which they moved. Ask for clues (give a list), hand-address the envelope and write "Important!!" and "Personal" on the outside (since many people throw away letters addressed to "occupant"), and include a self-addressed, stamped post card or ask them to call you collect. And ALWAYS mention that it's for a reunion.

If there is a forwarding order on file at the Post Office, any First Class mail with such a name and address will be forwarded automatically. However, if you write (or stamp) "Address Correction Requested" on the envelope, instead of being forwarded, the envelope will be returned to you along with the address correction. This will ensure that you will be notified of each forwarding address. However, you must pay 30 cents (1989) for each piece of mail returned in this way. In our opinion, it's worth the small investment. If you use this method, of course you should not write "Please Forward" on the envelope.

Include Everyone

Throughout your search keep in mind that it's important to include everyone. Don't forget those who didn't quite graduate or who had to drop out or move in their senior year. If someone in your class is presently overseas or in prison, or for some other reason obviously won't be able to attend, send him or her a notice anyway. Such people would especially appreciate knowing that they were thought of. Check your Junior yearbook, too, for those who may have moved away. Often such people feel a closer kinship with those they went to school with for 3 years than with the class they eventually graduated with. It's a sad fact that such people often don't get invited to the reunion that would be the most meaningful to them. Make an effort to locate as many people as possible, even though it may prove difficult and expensive. Remember, you are making an investment in future reunions as well as trying to make this one a great success.

Invite the Teachers

Teaching is a very difficult job with few rewards. Inviting the teachers to your reunion is a way of thanking them for their efforts. They invariably have a good time, not only with former students, but also with their former colleagues, some of whom they haven't seen in years. It's like a reunion within a reunion.

Finding teachers is almost the same as finding classmates, except for three things:

1. If they stayed in the teaching profession, they can usually be traced through the schools they taught at. This involves writing or calling each school in succession.

2. Your state's Teachers' Union will probably forward a letter if you include a stamped envelope. This should be good for both active and retired teachers.

3. Send a separate "missing" teachers list to all "found" teachers. Also send this list to your classmates—occasionally a student will stay in touch with a favorite teacher.

If yours is an older class, and there are only a few teachers still alive, then of course you would want to invite them as honored guests at no charge. However, under the more usual of circumstances with a lot of teachers involved, it may be prohibitive to not charge them. At least you should look carefully into the costs before deciding to charge them or not. And you should not consider it to be a breach of etiquette to ask them to pay. If it makes you feel better, you could ask them to pay for their "meal only," or offer a "teachers' discount."

It's appropriate to acknowledge the teachers during the program— it makes them feel welcome and appreciated. Don't forget to include them in your mailers, and to budget for this expense.

If the class before you invited them to their reunion the year before, don't worry about it—it's the gesture that counts. Some will still come and have a good time.

*　　　　*　　　　*　　　　*　　　　*

Sources for Finding People

This is by no means a complete list of the sources available to you, but for all practical purposes it's about all you will need for school reunions. The national level of sources (IRS, Social Security) has been left out because the person's social security number is required, and is not commonly known to school reunion organizers. For active duty or retired military personnel, see Chapter 12, "Military Reunions" and Appendix B. And for the best book that we know of on the subject, see the order form for *You Can Find Anyone* on p. 221.

Registrar of voters: This is by far the easiest and most productive public record to access, and it's free. Records are kept at the County level. Remember that most people live within 50 miles of where they grew up. If there is another county nearby, check those records, too.

Department of Motor Vehicles: Each state has its own name for this department. What you are looking for is the drivers license records. In most states this information, or at least the address and phone number, is available to the public. However, you will probably need the birthdate as well as the full name before they will conduct a search. There is almost always a charge ranging from 75¢ to $6 per search, regardless of whether the search is successful or not. The following states need either the person's written permission, or the driver's license number, which means that they are essentially hopeless: Alabama, Arkansas, Georgia, Hawaii, Idaho, Illinois, Iowa, Kansas, Missouri, and Pennsylvania. These states do not allow a driver's license check of any kind: Massachusetts and Washington (state). **(Dear readers: Please send us updated information for your area.)**

Title insurance firms: These are private companies with lots of information on people who own property within their state. It's not illegal for them to access this information for you, but they would be doing it as a favor. Be considerate and submit to them only 2 or 3 names at a time. Perhaps someone in your group works in such a firm.

County tax office or assessor's office: This is where the title insurance firms get their information, but of course they access all the counties of the state or in their area. These files are usually not computerized which means that you will have to physically look through the files. There is sometimes an hourly charge.

County Recorder's Office: Grantee/grantor records are held at the County level, and involve deeds, power of attorney papers, real estate transactions, liens, and anything officially recorded on paper between two or more people. When confronted with these files, don't be overwhelmed by the legal jargon, just make a note of the information that you can use, such as: addresses, full names, children's names, occupation, legal advisers, business partners, etc.

Marriage records: Most younger people take out their marriage license in the county where they grew up, and many women are married in their home community. This is at the County level and is especially good for finding women's married names. In some states, however, these records are "sealed."

Vital statistics records: Birth and death statistics start out at the County level, but a copy is usually sent to the State level. For local information, of course, go to the county courthouse. If you are dealing with a distant county or another state, then first try the Department of Health, the Department of Human Resources, or the Office of Vital Statistics (each state has a different name for it) at the state capitol. If they don't have the information you seek, they can tell you how to get it and how much it will cost. The fees range from $1 to $6 per search. In many cases, you will be checking these records to see if the person you are looking for has become a parent. If you do not know the children's first names, then you will be looking under the last name only. This approach will obviously work best if you are dealing with an unusual or uncommon last name. Also, since you are looking for a child (first name unknown) of the person you are actually looking for, you will probably have to do such a search in person rather than by mail.

Business license records: Recorded at the City and County level. About half the population eventually tries a business of their own.

A fictitious business name must be registered by anyone doing business under any name other than their given legal name.

PLEASE SEND US:

- more suggestions on how to find people.
- updates to the tips listed.
- tips that apply only to your particular area or state.
- an interesting real scenario of a "find" that you were involved in.

CHAPTER 7

The Filing System

*Definitions and Methods – Types of Files – Coding/Earmarking/
Lists – Categories of Information – About Computers – Mailing
Label Systems – Other Tips.*

In an attempt to describe all the possibilities, there is probably
more information in this chapter than you will need for your
particular situation. Please evaluate the possibilities presented
here, use the information that pertains to your needs, and discard
the rest. You should try for the simplest system that will still give
you what you want.

Definitions and Methods

You can collect and organize several useful categories of information during the course of your reunion. For groups and associations
that have reunions on a regular basis, this process is on-going and
unending. This chapter discusses the various methods of organizing
information and explains the categories that are possible and how
they are useful. The means of organizing and storing this information is referred to in this book as "the filing system." A "record" is
the information kept on one individual. A "file" is a group of
records.

Your records can be kept in one of three different ways:

1. On file cards—use 4 × 6 cards if your committee can put a lot of
   effort into finding people (more effort means more information
   which means you need the larger card); otherwise, use 3 × 5's.
   One name per card.

2. In a three ring binder—one name per sheet of paper. This is the best way (other than a computer) for reunion groups and associations that intend to put a lot of time and effort into finding people. Some "finds" may take several years and a lot of searching. In such cases, an 8 ½ × 11 binder system is much more efficient than a card system because it will hold a lot more information.

3. On computer disk—amazing things can be done on computers, but to go this route you will need someone who knows exactly what they are doing. This is no time to try something new. See "About Computers," p. 75.

Keep your files in alphabetical order by last name. Use the name you knew the person by. For instance, if a woman's married name is Smith, but you knew her as Mary Jane Doe, her entry would read: Mary Jane DOE Smith and would be alphabetized under the D's. Capitalizing or underlining her entire maiden name makes for easier reference. It can even appear on the mailing labels this way. This should get her immediate attention.

Types of Files

All records start off in the **original file** (see flow chart, Figure 6), and your intention is to eventually make this file as small as possible. All records here have either no address or an "improbable" address. If you are unsure of an address enough to not want to waste a stamp on it, then it's an "improbable" address. An example is an address that is 40 years old that you got from the school records. The chances are (although there are exceptions) that such an address is no longer good. The only reason that you would collect such an address in the first place would be if you have the time to personally go to the address and ask questions of the neighbors, or if you intend to search city directories (see p. 57). There is a slight chance that an old timer might know (or have a clue) where the person is or where they moved to.

As you can see from the flow chart, your system of filing can contain several branches or **sub-files.** From the original file the records go into either the mailing file or the deceased file. Once you have an address that you will mail to, the record goes into the mailing file which is divided into verified and unverified addresses.

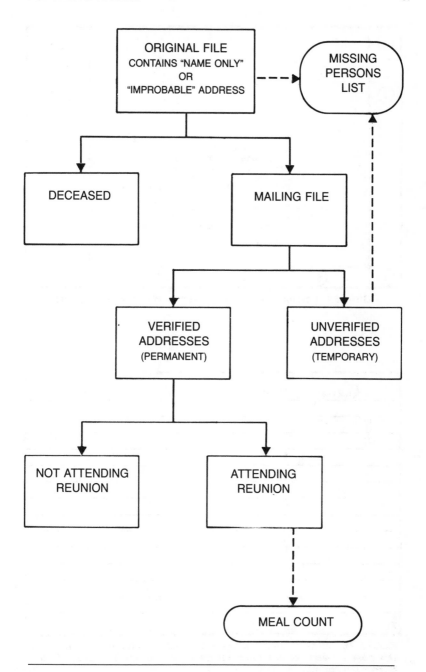

FIGURE 6. Flow chart for a basic reunion filing system.

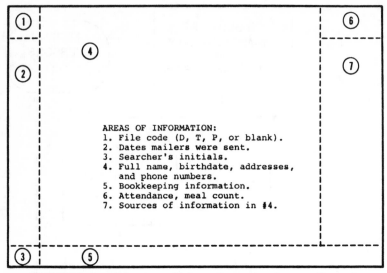

FIGURE 7A. *Possible areas of information and codes on a file card.*

AREAS OF INFORMATION:
1. File code (D, T, P, or blank).
2. Dates mailers were sent.
3. Searcher's initials.
4. Full name, birthdate, addresses, and phone numbers.
5. Bookkeeping information.
6. Attendance, meal count.
7. Sources of information in #4.

KAREN M. JONES

JW

FIGURE 7B. *All cards start out in the Original File with only the name. In this case a searcher has been assigned and her initials appear in the bottom left corner.*

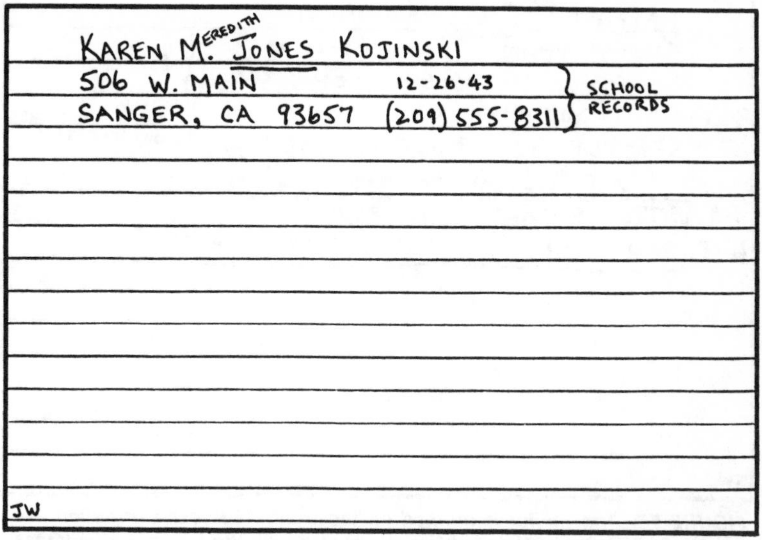

KAREN M. <u>JONES</u> KOJINSKI
506 W. MAIN   12-26-43   } SCHOOL
SANGER, CA 93657   (209) 555-8311   } RECORDS

JW

FIGURE 7C. The middle name, date of birth, and address and phone number at time of graduation were obtained from the school records. Someone remembers that she is married and that her name is now Kojinski. The maiden name is then underlined.

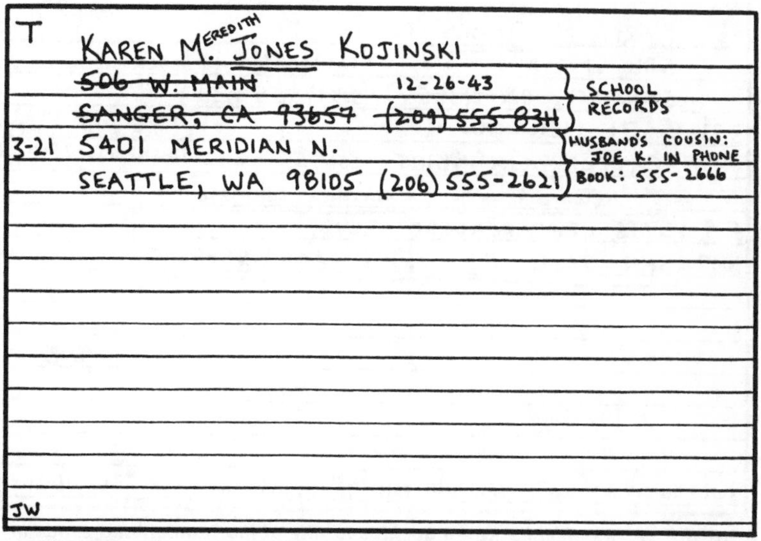

T   KAREN M. <u>JONES</u> KOJINSKI
     ~~506 W. MAIN~~   12-26-43   } SCHOOL
     ~~SANGER, CA 93657~~ ~~(209) 555-8311~~   } RECORDS
3-21 5401 MERIDIAN N.   HUSBAND'S COUSIN: JOE K. IN PHONE
     SEATTLE, WA 98105 (206) 555-2621   BOOK: 555-2666

JW

FIGURE 7D. The name Kojinski is found in the local phone book. It turns out to be the husband's cousin, Joe. Joe supplies an address and phone number in Seattle. A mailer is sent to the Seattle address on 3-21.

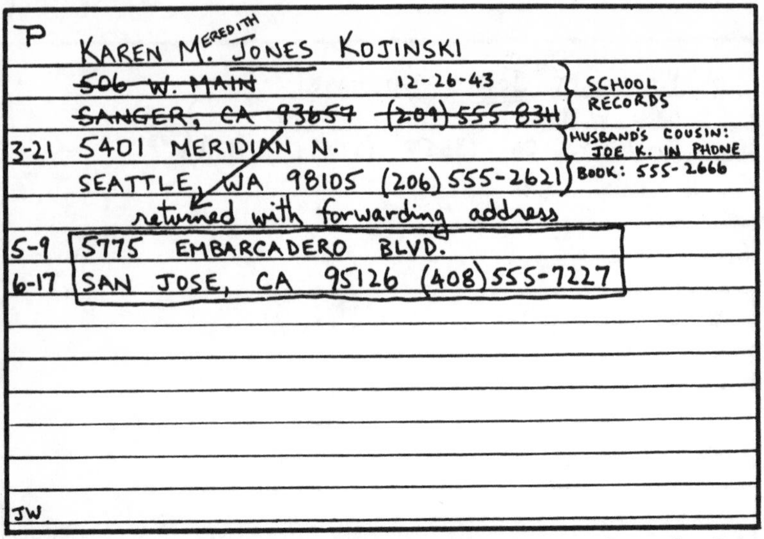

FIGURE 7E. *The mailer is marked on the front: "Address Correction Requested." The Post Office returns the mailer with the forwarding address (this service costs 30¢). The mailer is then sent to the San Jose address on 5-9. A second mailer (different from the first) is mailed on 6-17.*

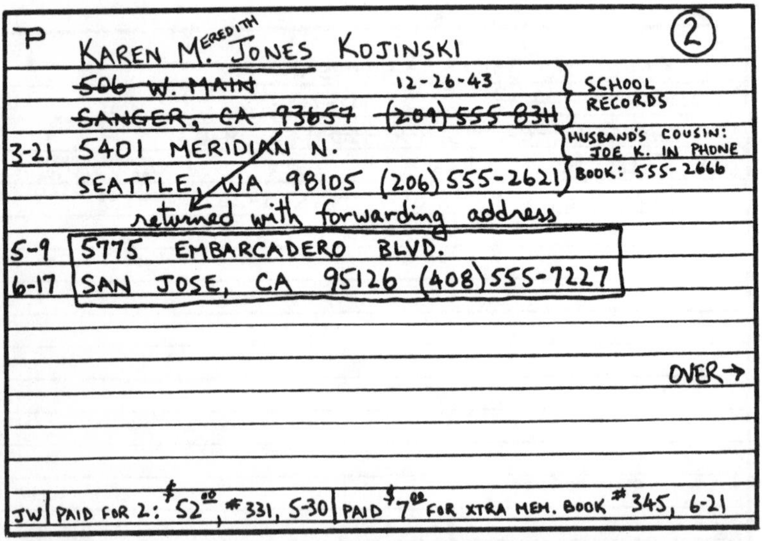

FIGURE 7F. *Meanwhile Karen decides to attend the reunion and sends in $52 for herself and her husband. The date of deposit and check number are recorded, and a circled "2" is written in the upper right corner. Then she learns from the second mailer that an extra memory book can be bought for $7. She sends in her $7 which is deposited on 6-21.*

```
-  WILL  BRING  OLD  MOVIES  ¦  PROJECTOR ⎫ PER PHONE CALL
-  ALSO  SENIOR  CLASS  SWEATER          ⎬      6-20
                                          ⎭       ↙
- SAYS:  JOHN  JORGENSON  IS  NOW  WORKING  FOR
         CHEVRON  IN  DUBLIN, CA.




  OCCUPATION :  HOUSEWIFE
  HUSBAND    :  RAY, TRUCK DRIVER
  KIDS       :  RALPH 17, CONNIE 13
  TRAVELED TO EUROPE IN '82
  HOBBIES :  CAMPING, TRAINING HORSES
```

FIGURE 7G. (Back of card.) On 6-20 she calls the committee chairperson and offers to bring some old movies, a projector, and a class sweater. She also has some info about John Jorgenson. The biographical information came from a survey sent out with the second mailer.

The verified addresses can further be divided into those attending the reunion and those not attending. (If teachers are invited, a similar file can be created for them.) The important thing to remember here is that these sub-files do not necessarily have to be physically separated from each other as long as they are marked or coded so that you can tell the status of each record at a glance (see "Coding/Earmarking/Lists," below). On the other hand, if your group is small and/or you have a good memory, you might favor the "separate sub-file" system (you can also separate out some sub-files and not others). The problem with separating the files comes when you want to check on the status of a particular individual and you can't remember exactly where the record might be. With separate files you will have to check more of the files in order to find the record. The general rules are: The fewer the sub-files (that are physically separated from each other), the easier it will be to find a particular record. And: The larger the group, the more you should try to keep your files consolidated. See "status list," below, for a tip on how to maintain large separated files.

All records in the **mailing file** have addresses you intend to mail to; therefore, the mailing information is derived directly from this file. There are two types of addresses in this file: verified and unverified. An address is unverified until you know for sure that it is accurate. (Remember: Just because the mailer doesn't come back by return mail, doesn't necessarily mean the addressee received it.) Unverified addresses plus the original file make up the missing person list.

Deceased file — try to learn the particulars. People are always wanting to know "how" and "when" a person died. This information can go into a memory book, can be posted at the reunion, or can part of a memorial display (see p. 121 and p. 132).

Coding/Earmarking/Lists

Coding is a means of marking a record or list by writing on it. Also, particular colors of ink or pencil can be used for certain categories of information. For example: red for bookkeeping information and green for mailing information. And, of course, the "position" of the code can be useful, too. See Figure 7A.

The upper left corner can contain a **file code** indicating which file the record is in. No code (blank) means the record is still in the original file. A deceased record is marked with a D. An unverified address is marked with a T (for Temporary), and a verified address has a P (for Permanent). A box is drawn around the verified address (use colored ink). Also, note that a T easily becomes a P without having to erase.

The **mailing date** in the left side margin indicates when the mailing was sent, and appears next to the address that the mailer was sent to. If two mailers are sent, two dates appear. If the person is "found" just before the reunion, and as a result both mailings are combined in one, the date is underlined twice.

The bottom left corner contains the **searcher's initials.** That way you always know who is in charge of finding the person. If a different searcher is assigned, put the new searcher's initials above the first.

Bookkeeping information can appear on the bottom line (or two) of a card or on one line near the bottom of a sheet of paper if you are using a three-ring binder system. It should contain the amount of payment, the check number, and the deposit date of each transaction, as well as the item paid for. This can serve as your itemized deposit record, if done faithfully (see p. 35 and Figure 7F).

Earmarking is a way of marking a record without writing on it. It can be done with paper clips (either the regular metal kind or the funny looking plastic kind), or colored self-stick dots. There are also plastic clips for file cards called "file card signals." These work somewhat like a paper clip, but stick up above the card. Also in this category are Post-It Tape Flags that come in bright colors, can be written on, and are removable. (For sources, see Appendix A, Dot Paste-Up Supply.) The position of the marker could also have a meaning. For example a paper clip on the left top of a card could mean one thing and on the right top could mean another. The same goes for color coding — most clips, including the metal ones, are available in colors. Possible reasons for earmarking: owes money, paid for memory book but can't attend, volunteered to work during reunion, candidate for an award (note of explanation should be attached), etc.

Several useful **lists** can be created from the files. These include: missing person list, deceased list, list of those attending the reunion, status list (see below), list of candidates for awards, list of those owing money, etc. For some lists it's important that the record also contain a note, code or earmark which indicates the category of the list. For example, as you add a name to the list of people attending the reunion, also be sure some type of code appears on that person's record. In this case, a circled number in the upper right hand corner would do. The number within the circle indicates the number of people attending—a "1" means the person is attending alone; a "2" means the person will have a guest; a "0" means the person will arrive after the dinner (adding these numbers gives you the meal count). Then if the list is lost, it can easily be re-created by finding all records with a circled number in the upper right corner.

The **status list** is a neat trick that is useful if you have a large group (and, therefore, large files) because it allows you to keep your files separated and still be able to quickly find the status of a particular record. It's simply a list of your group in alphabetical order (double space in case you need to add to it). Next to each name put the file code (see above). No code (blank) means it is still in the original file; a P means it is in the verified (Permanent) address file;

a T = unverified (Temporary) address file; D = deceased file. You could also put other coded information in this list, and thereby eliminate the need to create other lists. For example: the previously mentioned circled number could indicate that the person will be attending the reunion (see above); $X = owes money (write it in red); $B = can't attend but paid for memory book; etc. Of course, you can develop your own codes. Once you do so, write them out and pin them on your wall for easy reference. Again, always be sure an equivalent code or earmark appears on the record so that if the list is lost it can be re-created.

Other Information

Other categories of information that can be contained in or derived from these files:

1. "Tracing" information. When you collect information, write down everything: sources talked to, files checked, letters written, dead-ends followed, phone calls made, etc. Date each entry. You are leaving a "trace"—a running record or log of all the steps taken in order to find the person. Then, if the person disappears again, a "re-find" will be much easier, and dead-ends can be avoided. Serious reunion groups, such as many military and family associations, intentionally collect information for the purpose of more easily "re-finding" the person. Social security number, driver's license number, service number, birthdate, and next of kin (or "someone who will always know where you are") all fall under this category.

2. Indicate on the back of the record any names, tips, or clues that the person has given for finding other people. This source information is sometimes handy to know to follow up for more leads or to verify original information. Especially good for military reunions or any reunion where a lot of time and effort is put into finding people.

3. Biographical information—collected from surveys sent out, or occasionally from interviewing people on the phone. If using cards, put this info on the back (see Figure 7G). The amount of information can vary (see "Survey," end of Chapter 8). Minimum is "spouse's name," to be used for making name tags. File cards can hold only a small amount of info such as: spouse's name,

children's/grandchildren's names and ages, occupation, hobbies, highlights of the last 10 years. More information than this should be kept in a separate file like a three ring binder containing the returned survey sheets. If you are using a three ring binder system, then file the returned survey sheet behind the name sheet. There is no use in collecting more biographical information than you will actually use. An arrow or the word "over" can indicate that there is information on the back.

4. Notes on each individual about services and donations offered, skills that may come in handy, items that may be borrowed, etc.

5. Missing person list—a combination of the unverified address file and the original file. This should be updated and sent out with each and every mailing. It is not particularly important that it be in alphabetical order.

About Computers

Most filing systems are kept on file cards or in three ring binders. However, the personal computer is changing these somewhat old-fashioned methods. If there is any way you can make use of a home computer with a printer, by all means do so. BUT BE SURE the operator has "hands on" experience with both the computer and the software. This is no time to experiment. And ALWAYS have a "back up" system to protect your information.

A computer can streamline the whole process of creating, updating and maintaining your filing system. You will be able to insert each new address alphabetically with the push of a key. Biographical information, a missing person list, a list of those attending the reunion, a printed address list, or a meal count can be run off at any time. You are limited by the software and the experience and ability of the operator.

Quite often someone will have his or her secretary maintain the filing system or the mailing list on an office computer. But with such an arrangement the information is never "right at your fingertips," and it can be quite tedious to transfer information back and forth between you and the computer. "Access" is one of the key words in the world of computers. This means you, the user, should have direct access to the information at all times. The computer should be in the hands of the person most involved with the reunion, or maybe that person's good friend. But certainly not across town locked up in someone's office. If such an arrangement is your only choice, you would be far better off with an "old-fashioned" paper system.

Mailing Label Systems

If at all possible, address your mailers by hand. Figure one person per every 40–50 mailers and you should be done in an hour and a half at the most. This is by far the easiest way unless you are using a computer. However, if you can't get enough people together, or if you are running a long distance reunion and have no extra help (such as most military reunions), then you had better plan on some sort of address label system. There are basically two manual (non-computer) types:

1. Peel-off, self-sticking mailing labels come in sheets of 33 (3 across the top and 11 down). These sheets are the exact same size as a sheet of typing paper (8 ½ × 11) and can be photocopied onto (however, you may have to take your own labels to the copy shop). The usual method is to write or type each new address onto a plain white sheet of paper using a label template (see explanation below). Each label entry can be "generally" alphabetized by assigning a certain letter or letters to each sheet. Depending on the size of your class, you may have (for example) the A's, B's, and C's on one sheet or perhaps just the A's. Or you can assign one letter per row of 11 down, again depending on your situation. The names within each section do not necessarily have to be in alphabetical order. Just before each general mailing, the originals are photocopied onto labels which are then peeled off and stuck onto the mailers. Another use for these labels, by the way, is to paste one with a new address over the old address on the file cards. If it turns out that the old information becomes of interest again, the label peels off easily.

A **label template** comes with each package of labels that you buy. It is a regular size sheet of paper with heavy black lines printed on it to represent the label edges. When placed behind an ordinary sheet of white paper, the black lines show through to guide the placement of the addressing information onto the plain white sheet. The template is never written or typed on itself. It acts only as a guide.

2. The second method, which also makes use of self-sticking, peel-off labels, is a commercial set-up called CopyMaster. (Available at large office supply or stationery stores, or see Appendix A, Quill Corp.) CopyMaster consists of clear plastic pages (8 ½ × 11) with 33 pockets, and insert cards that fit into these pockets. The plastic pages (which have holes to fit into a three ring binder) and insert cards can be bought separately or in a package along with a binder and some address labels. The upper portion of the cards is for the mailing information and is the size of a mailing label. The lower portion, which is approximately the same size, is for any other information (see Figure 8). When the cards

RICHARD STONE
1055 Heaven Street
Cary, NC 27511

Betty   919/467-
2 boys   dob 1
golf   S8579
March 76   Art W.

FIGURE 8.

reside in their pockets, the lower portion doesn't show because the cards overlap each other. This allows for easy photocopying onto address labels. The best part of this system is that the file can always be kept in exact alphabetical order because the cards can be moved around (though it takes some time to do so).

For people who are not "found" until just before the reunion, don't bother using labels — simply hand-address their mailers. If you have more than one mailing, send these people all the mailings at one time; however, be sure to enclose a note of explanation to avoid confusion.

When copying onto labels, be sure to use a machine that copies at 100%. Many machines slightly magnify (around 102–103%) the original onto the copy. This can cause the copy to spill over the boundaries of the label, and you may end up with partial information on some labels (see Figure 9). This is especially true when making copies of copies. The fancier machines have the option of copying at 100%, but you may have to ask for it.

If a previous reunion has left you with no file cards, but only a batch of labels or label originals (created using a template), you can create a new card file by photocopying onto new labels, sticking these labels onto cards, and alphabetizing the cards.

The **etiquette** involved in addressing envelopes for a school reunion that is scheduled "occasionally" (every five years or every ten years, for example) is to address it to the class member only, not

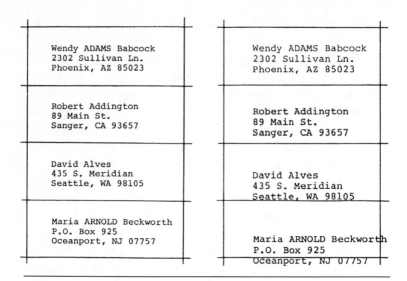

FIGURE 9. *Because some photocopy machines make copies that are slightly larger than the originals, making copies from copies can result in addresses over-spilling their bounds. Always copy from the original or at 100%.*

including the spouse's name. A woman's maiden name should be included. The invitation should, of course, make it clear that the spouse is invited. If you have reunions every year or two, organized by an association or long-standing committee, then over the years a rapport may develop between some of the spouse's and the members of the committee. When the spouse becomes known to the committee, then the envelopes should be addressed to both, as if he or she were part of the "family." In such cases where the woman is the group member, then the woman's name should appear first: "Mary and Donald Jones." With these frequently occuring reunions, it is not necessary to include the woman's maiden name unless she has retained it. Including the "title of address" (Mr., Mrs., Miss, Ms.) is not absolutely necessary. Reunions are informal affairs as compared to weddings and graduations.

Other Tips

- The less you copy and re-copy information, the better. Stick with the original record; cross out the old info and add the new. Don't erase—the old info may prove useful if all other leads die out.

(Old information is especially useful to future reunions because if the person "disappears" again, the old sources will be the most likely to help relocate the person.) If the front and back of the card become full, add a second card (perhaps of a different color) in front of the first and paper-clip them together. If you are using paper clips for an earmarking system, then staple them together.

- Be sure to save all information for the next reunion. Keep one person in charge of it, preferably someone who will not be moving around a lot. And give copies of the address and phone number list to two or three other people for safe keeping. Announce who is in charge of the address list in your mailings and at the reunion so that people can send change-of-address announcements to that person between reunions. Also, have copies of the address list available at the reunion along with scratch paper so people can copy the addresses of classmates they would like to stay in touch with.

- As your file grows and contains more and more information (especially bookkeeping information), it becomes more valuable. It would be a real disaster if it disappeared the week before the reunion. We have heard all kinds of horror stories from children throwing it out the car window to committee members forgetting who last borrowed it. TAKE GOOD CARE OF IT. Don't loan it out—not even a portion of it. All of the information, even if just a name, is valuable. If someone wants to try their luck at finding some people, don't give them the records, not even the ones that contain only the names and no other information. Give them a list of the names instead, or a separate copied group of records, but NEVER the original set. If your information is on computer disk, INSIST that the operator frequently update the back-up copy.

- Address labels, file card trays (metal or plastic and in 3 sizes), and file cards (lined, plain, and in colors) are available from Quill Corp. See Appendix A.

CHAPTER 8

Mailers and Newsletters

*Newsletters – Mailers Are Important – Contents of the Mailers –
Creating the Mailers – Tips on Graphics – Other Embellishments –
Return Address/Rubber Stamps – Postage – Desktop Publishing –
The Survey.*

Newsletters

The term "mailer," as used in this book, refers to the notices sent
out before a particular reunion — announcing, describing, and explaining that reunion. A newsletter, on the other hand, is a more
general form of communication that comes out on a (more or less)
continuing basis with the role of acting as a small newspaper for the
group as a whole. Such a newsletter does not necessarily have
anything to do with a reunion. This chapter concentrates on mailers, but much of the information will apply to newsletters as well.
Certainly the tips on how to create them will be the same. Your
local library is a good place for further information — there is no
lack of printed material on the subject. Also check some of the
reference books mentioned in Appendix A.

Mailers Are Important

The only link between most of your classmates and the reunion
will take place through the mail. All of the impressions, notions,
ideas, and opinions that will be formed about the upcoming reunion, whether good, bad, or indifferent will come from these pieces
of paper that are sent out. They will be read and scrutinized very
carefully, and will probably carry much more weight and import
than the sender ever intended. The thing about reunion notices
getting casually tossed into the trash like junk mail is a myth. They

may wind up in the trash, but only after serious consideration.

The first reaction that some people have upon reading their reunion invitation is that they won't go. Then, over the period of weeks or months before the event, they talk themselves into going, or their friends or spouse talk them into going. An invitation that is carelessly worded, has missing or incorrect information, or looks sloppy gives the impression that the reunion is going to turn out the same way, and gives the reader a real good excuse to say, "no thanks." We assure you that time spent to produce high quality, thoughtfully-worded mailers is worth every effort. They will not only help your reunion succeed socially but economically as well. The more people who attend, the more people there are to share the costs, and, therefore, the less it will cost per person.

Many mailers are very efficient in style, short and to the point, and some reunions send out only one. Essentially, they are little more than an invitation with the date, time, place, cost, a registration form, and perhaps the "type of dress" and the missing person list. They give the necessary information and get back the necessary responses. This is fine for those who don't have time to do more, but in the long run we don't believe it's the most effective method.

We recommend two mailers because it's a better way to deal with the psychology of getting a diverse and scattered group of people to respond. The first should come out 5 to 6 **months** before the event, the second 6 to 8 **weeks** before. An advance notice of 5 to 6 months should give people plenty of time to plan their vacations — this is especially important for the long-distance folks — and to save the necessary money. It gives those who are a bit uneasy about reunions a chance to think things over and get psyched up, and it allows plenty of time for finding people. The second mailer reminds people, and gives last minute changes and additional information.

We encourage something like a small newsletter. Of course, this requires some people in your group who have the time and interest to produce it. It could contain newsy, interesting information, such as: a list of committee members, what type of program and facility the committee is considering, how they are going about finding people, and so on. It can solicit comments and suggestions or ask for volunteers and donated items. Such a friendly approach generates interest and conveys the feeling that the committee is really involved and trying to do a good job. This will definitely get more people to attend, especially those who are on the borderline, and will lend a warmer atmosphere to the reunion itself. School reunions, like weddings and family reunions, are more attractive to people if they are not treated in the business-like manner of conventions. Show your best writer the examples in this chapter and you are certain to come up with something presentable.

Contents of the Mailers

There are basically two parts to the mailers:

1. The essential facts, figures, and information.
2. The newsy, chatty notes and articles that lend a friendly style, but are not absolutely necessary.

What to put in the first mailer:

(To be mailed out 5 to 6 months before the reunion. Choose the items from the "optional" list that fit your situation and discard the rest.)

Essential:

● date, time and location of the reunion.

● cost per person (approximate or exact).

● missing person list.

● return address.

● registration form (if you want to start receiving money).

(NOTE: For an example of a Registration Form, see the end of this chapter.)

Optional (but recommended that some be included):

● request for deposit or announcement of discount for early reservations.

● how to make out the check.

● list of committee members with phone numbers.

● short history of decisions made and those in progress.

- solicit comments and suggestions on: type of music; band, DJ, or tape?; photographers; type of dress; etc.
- get ideas for the program, award categories and prizes.
- include a survey.
- ask for volunteers and donations (give list of what is needed: MC for program, slide projector, taped music, door prizes, etc.).
- ask for old photos, slides, movies, school sweaters, and other memorabilia.
- ask for information on "missing" classmates.
- give name, address, and phone number of person in charge of mailing list so people can send change-of-address cards in the future.
- provide names, phone numbers, and rates of a few motels in the area.
- give approximate date of the next mailer.
- explain refunding rules.
- include jokes, cartoons, interesting trivia, and historical data.
- deadlines (if any).

What to put in the second mailer:
(To be mailed out 6 to 8 weeks before the reunion.)

Essential:
- date, time, and location.
- exact cost per person.
- how to make out the check.
- registration form.
- request for remainder of fee from those who sent deposits (if this was your original policy).
- updated list of "missing" classmates.
- type of dress.
- return address.

Optional (but recommended that some be included):

- updated information from the first mailer, last minute news, details, changes or additions to original plans.

- encouragement for borderliners and procrastinators (if your class isn't too large, a list of those planning to attend will often entice others).

- description of program, type of music, food.

- request for volunteers and donations (give a list of what is still needed).

- ask for information on "missing" classmates.

- survey (for those who were found late and did not get the first mailing).

- names, phone numbers, and rates of motels in the area.

- refunding rules.

- deadlines (if any).

- more jokes, cartoons, interesting trivia, and historical data.

NOTE: There may be other items to include in the mailers which will pertain only to your reunion.

In the preliminary stages, when you are just getting started and are not even sure if there will be a reunion, you can have mailers of a completely different nature. They can be used, for example:

1. to take a poll of your class to see if there is enough interest in a reunion. If so, what type?

2. to announce that a committee is forming, ask for volunteers and ideas, and announce time, date, and place of the first meeting.

Creating the Mailers

First, you need to spend time thinking and planning. Make a list of all essential facts and figures. Double check to be sure you have included ALL the necessary information. If people in your group wish to write short articles, explain the length you want, and give them a definite deadline. Unless you like to compose on the typewriter, you will probably write your first draft longhand. Look over this draft for changes and corrections, rewrite where needed, and

then type it. Once you have a typed version, have someone else
look it over for final editing and to be sure you haven't left anything
out.

Figures 10A and 10B show the difference between a regular
reunion mailer and one that has been put into a newsletter format.
The wording is the same in both, and the same typewriter was used.
The difference is some clip art, some "rub-on" type, a vertical line,
and a trip to the copy shop for the reduction. It's really not that hard
to do. See "Tips on Graphics" for more information.

```
Regular typing looks like this.  It is
large, takes up a lot of space and looks
like a business letter. To dress up your
mailers or newsletters, you can try some
of the following tricks:
```

```
    Columnize your format. If the fi-
    nal result will be printed on
    8 1/2 x 11 paper, then two column-
    s side by side are probably best.
    If you have a 1/2" margin on both
    sides plus a 1/2" between columns,
    then each column will be 3 1/2"
    wide. Elite type looks better un-
    less you have it reduced (below).


    And if you have your original type reduc-
    ed down to 80% it will look even better.
    But to get the final result 3 1/2" wide,
    that means your original should be 4 3/8"
    wide (use a calculator). So type it up
    then take it down to a copy shop and have
    it reduced to 80%. It'll cost about a
    quarter. Bring it back and paste it up
    and add some other interesting things
    like separators and borders and clip art,
    all of which you can find at an art store
    that has graphic supplies. But you can
    also use asterisks for separators, like
    this:


    *        *        *        *        *
```

```
or just draw a short line like this:
```

```
or throw in a fancy store-bought one like
this:
```

---◆---

Another neat trick is to capitalize the first letter of each article by using some "rub on" type or transfer lettering that you can get at the art store. Make sure you get the right size letters by typing a couple of lines on your typewriter and taking them down to the art store for measurement. A letter that's a little too big looks better than one that's too small. You can also apply the letter after it's been reduced.

YOU CAN START OFF EACH ARTICLE with about a half line of capitalized type. The capitalized part should be a complete phrase or idea, not just chopped off anywhere.

For the final draft, it's best to use a professional quality typewriter, preferably with a carbon ribbon. If your typewriter uses only fabric ribbons, put in a fresh ribbon and clean out the o's and e's. You want a crisp, dark print that will reproduce well. If you have a choice, "Letter Gothic" from IBM is ideal. Stay away from "Script" type faces. They are popular, but they don't reproduce well and they become tedious to read. If you have any secretaries, typesetters, printers, or graphic artists in your group, ask for their help. Obviously, the fewer sheets of paper you mail out, the cheaper, but don't crowd it too much. If necessary, go to the larger legal size paper. You can liven it up with clip art and rub-on type (see "Tips on Graphics"). When creating the originals, type on only **one** side of a sheet of paper. It will be "backed" (printed on both sides of one sheet) at the printer's or copy shop. If you are doing any "cutting and pasting," use paste-up (layout) boards for a guide. They are very inexpensive (about 50¢ each), and have guide lines printed in "non-repro" blue ink. Available at graphic art stores. See Figure 11.

Quick printing or photocopying is the next step. Unless you are mailing a very small quantity, quick printing may be less expensive and probably better looking, especially if you are including photographs. One exception is the latest models of Xerox copiers—they give excellent results. But get several bids and **be sure to compare quality.** (See the

January 1989

Dear Friends:

Can you believe that it's really been 30 years since we all graduated together at Sanger High? Amazing! But now we have a chance to be together once more -- if only for an evening. Our 30th reunion will take place at the Washington Country Club on Saturday, August 12, 1989. Mark that down on your calendar right now, 'cause we'd really like to see you. The doors will open at 6 p.m. with a no-host bar. Dinner is at 8, followed by a short program, and dancing and conversation until 2 a.m. We're trying to keep the cost under $30 per person, but will let you know for sure in our next mailing.

In order to get some "start up" money for our reunion we are making a special offer. Anyone who sends us $20 before April 1 gets a $5 discount on the admission price to the reunion. And, of course, we won't turn down any donations either. Make out checks to: "Sanger High Class of '59 Reunion," and remember to mail them before April 1. Thanks a lot.

If you have any questions regarding the reunion, call or write: Junior Alvarez, 3323 S. Oak St., Sanger, CA 93657, 209/555-2933.

If you have information on any of the "missing" people, or can volunteer to help find people, call or write: Ron Jacobs, 1561 Main St., Fresno, CA 93712, 209/555-7768.

FIGURE 10A. This is a portion of a typical reunion mailer. See Fig. 10B.

Reunion News

SPECIAL REUNION EDITION
Volume 1, Number 1
January, 1989

THE GANG'S GETTING TOGETHER

Can you believe that it's really been 30 years since we all graduated together at Sanger High. Amazing! But now we have a chance to be together once more -- if only for an evening. Our 30th reunion will take place at the Washington Country Club on Saturday, August 12, 1989. Mark that down on your calendar right now, 'cause we'd really like to see you. The doors will open at 6 p.m. with a no-host bar. Dinner is at 8, followed by a short program, and dancing and conversation until 2 a.m. We're trying to keep the cost under $30 per person, but we will let you know for sure in our next mailing.

☞ IF YOU HAVE ANY QUESTIONS
    REGARDING THE REUNION, CALL OR
    WRITE: Junior Alvarez, 3323 S. Oak
St., Sanger, CA 93657, 209/555-2933.

HELP!

IN ORDER TO GET some "start-up" money for our reunion we are making a special offer. Anyone who sends us $20 before April 1 gets a $5 discount on the admission price to the reunion. And, of course, we won't turn away any donations either. Make out checks to: "Sanger High, Class of '59 Reunion," and remember to mail them before April 1. Thanks a lot.

  *   *   *   *   *

⬆ IF YOU HAVE INFORMATION ON ANY OF THE
    "MISSING" PEOPLE, OR CAN VOLUNTEER TO
    HELP FIND PEOPLE, CALL OR WRITE: Ron
Jacobs, 1561 Main St., Fresno, CA 93712,
209/555-7768.

❖ ❖ ❖ ❖ ❖ ❖ ❖ ❖

FIGURE 10B. This is the same mailer as Fig. 10A, but put into a newsletter format. The same typewriter and wording was used in both. The difference is some clip art, some transfer lettering, and a photocopy reduction.

Yellow Pages under "Printers," or "Copying and Duplicating Services.") Both standard (8 ½ × 11) and legal (8 ½ × 14) size paper will be available. Also, some copiers will now do 11 × 17 which can be folded in half to make a nice looking newsletter. Colored papers are available at a slightly higher cost. Don't use coin-operated copy machines, the kind you find in libraries and supermarkets. They are more expensive, the quality can be terrible, and they don't copy onto both sides of the same sheet. "Home copiers" are poor quality, too, although they will copy onto both sides of the same sheet by putting the paper through twice.

Once the printing is done, you can set up a work party to stamp, fold, and address the mailers. (For a price, the folding can be done by the print shop.) You can use envelopes or simply fold the mailers in thirds and staple or tape them shut (also see p. 99, "Return Address"). The maximum size for First Class Mail, by the way, is 6 ⅛" × 11 ½" after it's folded. If the piece is folded, it must be stapled or taped shut to qualify for First Class Mail. Have plenty of label-peelers and stamp-lickers (actually, use a sponge) available so the work will go quickly. Older children might be enticed (coerced?) into helping with this job.

Tips on Graphics
(See Appendix A for helpful books, catalogs and suppliers.)

- You can get more printing onto a sheet of paper by reducing the size of the original down to 75–80%. This can be done photographically for $4–5 per photo, or on some photocopying machines for about 25¢ per copy. The quality won't be as good with photocopying, but it will be adequate. Make the original the proper size so that the reduced copy fits into the required space. For example: an original of 10″ × 10″ when reduced down to 80% will be 8″ × 8″ (100% means the same size).

- 11 × 17 folded in half comes out to 8½ × 11. This makes a nice newsletter size that can be opened like a magazine. The printing shop can fold it for you at extra cost.

- "Rub-on" type and transfer lettering can be bought at graphics supply stores. These can be used to create letterheads, headlines, or any "line of type" that is to appear in large or stylized letters. They come in hundreds of styles and many sizes. Graphic art stores have catalogs that you can peruse at home at your leisure. It's much too confusing to pick a type style at the store.

- Kroy lettering machines are now available for customer use at some copy shops. These machines put out a tape of "headlines" in different styles and sizes of type. The operator turns a wheel that points to each letter in succession, and slowly but surely the heading is created. Prices are very inexpensive, starting at about 30¢ per inch.

- "Clip art" is any line image (not half-tone or photograph) that can be used to enhance a printed work. The most common example is the hand with pointing finger. See Figure 12 for examples. These usually come in books or sheets, available at graphic art stores. You clip them out (hence the name) and paste them onto your "original." However, the cheapest source is magazines and newspapers—sometimes not legal, but certainly a minor offense. If you find something you like, but it's the wrong size, it can be made larger or smaller by using photocopiers with the ability to enlarge or reduce. Other clip art examples are: decorative borders, banners, frames, arrows, symbols, etc. A catalog will give you more ideas. Send for catalogs from Dot Paste-Up Supply, The Printers Shopper, or the manufacturer (see Appendix A).

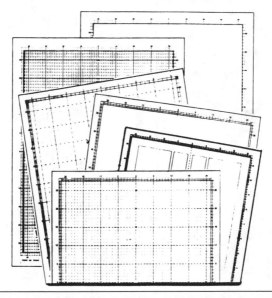

FIGURE 11. *Layout boards are one of the secrets to creating professional looking mailers and newsletters. There are many different grids and weights, but all are printed in "non-repro" blue (here depicted in black). Available in graphic art stores or from Dot Paste-Up Supply (see Appendix A).*

FIGURE 12. Clip art and transfer lettering go a long way toward making your mailers and newsletters look more interesting. Examples like these and thousands more are available from graphic art stores and mail order suppliers (see Appendix A). It is not legal to copy the images on this page.

- Any image (clip art, photos, borders, headings) can be enlarged or reduced in a photocopy machine. The trick is to find the right machine. Some machines reduce only. Some have only two or three settings (for example: 64%, 78%, and 120%). Some have incremental settings of 1% or ½%. All of them have range limits (for example: 64–142%). The Kodak IM40 will go from 36–400%. Since you want to stay away from copies of copies as much as possible (especially with photos), call around to find a machine that will give you what you want in one "shot." The better copy shops have several machines available, each one specializing in a different function.

- Most photocopiers are designed to not "see" the color blue. This can be a problem when trying to photocopy letters written in (or signed in) blue ink (see Figure 13). The best cure is prevention. When soliciting letters that will be reproduced, give instructions to not use blue ink. Red ink is okay since it shows up as black. If it's just a signature, you can try to carefully trace over it with black ink. Otherwise, try to find a photocopy machine that can "see" blue. Also, setting the contrast control for "darker" can help.

- If you can't get good results when photocopying photos, try using a "copy screen." This is a transparent plastic film with tiny white dots that break up the solid blackness in the photo. It's laid directly under the photo in the copy machine. The better copy shops will have these, but call first. Otherwise, they can be purchased at graphic art stores. Some of the very latest copy machines now have a "photo" setting. This makes use of an internal type of copy screen.

- If you are including photos in a mailer or newsletter, the quality will turn out better if you use the quick-print method instead of photocopying.

- Color photos can be made into black-and-white, but the results are always a little muddy. The photo of the cake on p. 129 is an example of an original color photo made into black-and-white. Anytime that photos are taken that will be reproduced in black-and-white (for newspaper publicity, memory book, etc.), always use black-and-white film.

- When getting multiple copies done at a copy shop, ALWAYS check the first copy for shadow lines, specks, mis-alignment, etc., before giving the go-ahead on the others. (See Figure 13.) Take a bottle of white- out with you to make corrections. Copy shops don't keep white-out around because some people forget to let it dry and it gums up the machine or glass. If shadow lines or specks appear on the first copy, then use the white-out on the original and try another single copy. If they persist, ask the operator if the machine can be adjusted for contrast or if there is another machine in the shop that has a better contrast adjustment. Be absolutely certain that the first copy is what you want before giving the go-ahead on the others. If you can't get what you want, try another copy shop—there is an amazing difference in quality among different brands and models of copy machines. Another factor that affects quality is how long it's been since the last routine maintenance of the machine.

- The 1025 and 1035 model Xerox copiers have interchangeable color cartridges (green, blue, red, brown and black). This allows you (for example) to have a color heading with black text (by putting the paper through the machine twice). The originals are all in black—it's the changeable cartridges that produce the different colors. However, these machines are getting harder to find. If interested, call around first. (Note: This is not a "color copier.")

Reunion News

SPECIAL REUNION EDITION
Volume 1, Number 1
January, 1989

THIS IS A PHOTOCOPY OF BLUE INK

FIGURE 13. Problems and "mistakes" such as these can easily be avoided. Use "white-out" on specks and shadow lines. Use a layout board and a triangle to properly align the "paste-up." Avoid blue ink. When doing multiple copies, always check the first copy very carefully before giving the "go ahead" on the others.

Cutting and pasting your "original" together to get it ready for the printer or photocopier is called "paste-up." Graphic artists who do this for a living have all sorts of expensive equipment, most of which you don't need. However, it helps to have:

- paste-up (layout) boards, base sheets, or planning paper. These are printed with "non-repro blue" guide lines, and are used to create and paste-up the original. They come in different weights, sizes, and grids (hence the different names), and are useful for aligning the work properly (see Figure 11). The best selection is from Dot Paste-Up Supply, and their catalog tells you everything you need to know (see Appendix A). However, their minimum order is 100 sheets. Small quantities are available from graphic art stores.

- a triangle with a right angle. This is to get the copy lined up level, and to provide a straight edge for the razor blade.

- razor blades (single edge).

- scissors.

- a blue pencil. Used to make marks or notes on the original that won't show up on the final result. Ask for a non-repro blue pencil (not pen) at a graphic arts store.

- white-out. Liquid, comes in a small bottle, apply with brush. Commonly used for typing errors. Will get rid of "shadow lines" that are the result of the edges of paper layers showing up in the photocopy.

- something to cut on when you use the razor blade. Don't use the kitchen table or anything else you don't want to mark up. Use masonite (hardboard), good quality plywood without knots or cracks, glass, marble, etc. Glass works best.

- masking tape. Used to hold down the original while you are working on it.

- glue, tape (transparent), wax, or spray adhesive. Used to hold the various pieces down on the original. With glue or tape, it's difficult to pick up a piece and re-set it (in case you make a mistake or change your mind). Professionally it's done with wax because wax allows you to pick up a piece and re-set it as many times as you like. However, the cheapest little hand-held waxer is $45 (they are electric in order to melt the wax)—a good investment if you want to afford it. But for one reunion's worth of work, or one or two newsletters a year, the best bet is either a wax stick (like a lipstick) for around $3, or non-permanent spray mount adhesive for about $10 per can.

Or you might consider the "Office Paste-Up Kit" offered by Dot Paste-Up Supply for around $60. It includes all of the above plus some. See Appendix A.

Other Embellishments

It's fun for the reader as well as the editor to include trivia, sayings, proverbs, quotes, jokes, birthdays (of group members and celebrities), historic dates, bits of wisdom, recipies, quizzes, puzzles, brain teasers, and items of nostalgic or historic interest (especially if they compare the past with the present). There are many books that can help you with such information. Some are listed in Appendix A, but many more can be found in your local library. There are also subscription services that provide such information and clip art to newsletter editors on a monthly basis (Appendix A, Fillers for Publications). This would be extravagant for most of you, but large military and family associations may well benefit from such a subscription. Also, the Master of Ceremonies of your reunion program may be interested in some of this material. See "The Program" in Chapter 10 for ways in which it can be used.

The editors of many military and family association newsletters think of their job as a hobby. They enjoy collecting and organizing material for the next issue. This can involve soliciting recipies and birthdays from members of their group, taking their own black-and-white photos, writing a column, creating trivia quizzes and puzzles, researching in libraries, etc. Many of these people are retired and have the time to volunteer. You may not have the time or interest to be so involved, but for a one- or two-time mailer or an annual or bi-annual newsletter, the research time is miniscule. One or two hours of time spent in a library will yield enough information for a couple of issues. And you will be amazed at the difference in your mailer or newsletter.

There are companies now that offer "historical printouts of any date." The time span is usually from 1900 to present, and the main purpose is to show people what was happening when they were born. These companies are mainly mail order, but can sometimes be found set up at county and local fairs. The price is certainly right ($2–3 per printout, 8 ½ × 11 sheet). The printout of your graduation date will give you enough information for one or two mailers or newsletters. Figure 14 shows an example. See Appendix A, Window In Time, for a source.

WINDOW IN TIME

DECEMBER 26, 1943

DECEMBER

THIS IS HOW THE CALENDAR WOULD LOOK ON DECEMBER 26, 1943

S	M	T	W	T	F	S
			1	2	3	4
5	6	7	8	9	10	11
12	13	14	15	16	17	18
19	20	21	22	23	24	25
26	27	28	29	30	31	

PRESIDENT OF THE U.S. WAS FRANKLIN D. ROOSEVELT
VICE-PRESIDENT WAS HENRY A. WALLACE

SOME PRICES IN 1943, COMPARED WITH 1986 ARE:

	1943	1986
A POUND LOAF OF BREAD	$0.09	$0.70
A HALF GALLON OF MILK	$0.31	$1.18
A POUND OF BUTTER	$0.53	$2.65
A POUND OF ROUND STEAK	$0.44	$2.69
ONE GALLON OF GASOLINE	$0.17	$1.07
A NEW FORD AUTOMOBILE	N.A.	$8,725.
AVERAGE ANNUAL INCOME	$1,951.	$21,310.

IN 1943 - THE WORLD SERIES WAS WON BY THE NEW YORK YANKEES (AL)
BEATING THE ST. LOUIS CARDINALS (NL)

MOST
POPULAR:
SONG - OH, WHAT A BEAUTIFUL MORNIN - ALFRED DRAKE
MOVIE - CASABLANCA
ACTOR - PAUL LUKAS - "WATCH ON THE RHINE"
ACTRESS - JENNIFER JONES - "THE SONG OF BERNADETTE"

SOME STORIES THAT APPEARED IN NEWSPAPERS ON OR NEAR DECEMBER 26, 1943 ARE:

12/24   GENERAL DWIGHT D. EISENHOWER WAS NAMED SUPREME COMMANDER OF THE
        EUROPEAN INVASION FORCES.

12/27   THE HEISMAN MEMORIAL TROPHY, FOR THE OUTSTANDING COLLEGIATE
        FOOTBALL PLAYER OF THE YEAR, WAS AWARDED TO ANGELO BERTELLI THE
        QUARTERBACK FOR NOTRE DAME. NOTRE DAME WAS THIS YEAR'S NATIONAL
        COLLEGE FOOTBALL CHAMPIONS.

1/7   FRANK SINATRA, THE IDOL OF THE "BOBBY-SOXERS," BEGINS AN
        ENGAGEMENT IN MANHATTAN'S PARAMOUNT THEATER BEFORE A SCREAMING
        AUDIENCE OF 30,000.

1/16   PAPER SHORTAGES CAUSED PUBLISHERS TO COME OUT WITH PAPERBACK
        BOOKS. THE POPULARITY WAS SO GREAT THAT THE PRACTICE NEVER
        ENDED.

FIGURE 14. Historical printouts are available by mail (see Appendix A). They can provide you with good information to include in your mailers, newsletters, or reunion program.

Examples of trivia:
When we graduated:
The price of gas was _____ per gallon.
We mailed a letter for _____.
Bread cost _____ per loaf.
The ballpoint pen was not yet invented.
Credit cards did not exist.
The Zip Code was 10 years in the future.
We used slide rules instead of calculators in math class.
Life magazine was _____ per copy.

Examples of quotes and sayings:
"At age 20, we worry about what others think of us. At 40, we don't care what they think of us. At 60, we discover they haven't been thinking of us at all."
"Reconciling the past in order to be at ease with the present is necessary to gaining wisdom."
"The hardest thing about a reunion is holding in your stomach for six hours."

Examples of quizzes and puzzles: (See Figure 15.)
Using almanacs and encyclopedias for "What Year Was It?" is too slow (with the exception of encyclopedia annual volumes). The best chronology resources are *The Timetables of History* and *The People's Chronology*, both described in Appendix A. The best sources for a quiz are trivia books and games.

WHIZ QUIZ

What word contains the vowels in order?
– a – e – i o u –

(facetious)

WHAT YEAR WAS IT?

Pennsylvania Turnpike completed from Carlisle to Irwin. A new Chevy coupe sells for $659. Color TV pioneered by CBS. Reds win first Series, first nylon stockings go on sale. "You are my sunshine" popular. Kate Hepburn stars in "Philadelphia story", Ralph Edwards introduces "Truth or Consequences".

(1940)

WHIZ QUIZ

John was standing directly behind Mary. Mary was standing directly behind John
Same Mary - Same John.
But how can that be?

(John and Mary were standing back to back)

WHAT YEAR WAS IT?

Margaret Thatcher new leader of England. Suez Canal reopens. Astronauts and Cosmonauts share meals 140 miles in space. Philadelphia Flyers win Stanley cup. Art Carney Oscars for Best Actor. Salmon spawn in Connecticut River, 1st time in 100 years.

(1975)

FIGURE 15. *Here are two ways to make your mailers or newsletters more interesting. The answers, of course, should appear on a different page than the questions.*

FIRST-CLASS POSTAGE
Rate for one-ounce letters

July 1, 1885	2 cents	May 16, 1971	8 cents
Nov. 3, 1917	3 cents	March 2, 1974	10 cents
July 1, 1919	2 cents	Dec. 31, 1975	13 cents
July 6, 1932	3 cents	May 29, 1978	15 cents
Aug. 1, 1958	4 cents	March 22, 1981	18 cents
Jan. 7, 1963	5 cents	Nov. 1, 1981	20 cents
Jan. 7, 1968	6 cents	Feb. 17, 1985	22 cents

```
                    (prices given in cents)
                    1920    1930    1940    1950    1960    1970    1980

1 lb. loaf of bread 11.5    8.6     8.0     14.3
½ gal. of milk      33.4    28.2    25.6    41.2
1 doz. eggs         68.1    44.5    33.1    60.4
1 lb. coffee        47.0    39.5    21.2    79.4
1 gal. gasoline     29.8    20.0    18.4    26.8    31.1    35.7    119
```

FIGURE 16. As you come across charts like these (or other trivia information) in newspapers or magazines, clip and save them. They can provide useful information for your reunion program or newsletter. For example a Class of 1963 could say: "We mailed our graduation notices for 5¢"; or create a question: "Do you remember what it cost to mail our graduation notices?"

Return Address/Rubber Stamps

If you are folding the sheets in thirds for mailing instead of using envelopes, you can have the return address printed in the upper left corner of your mailer's "mailing face" (the appropriate third of your outside sheet) and "First Class Mail" and "Address Correction Requested" printed in the bottom left corner. Include a phone number along with the return address. Or, you can order pre-printed, self-stick, peel-off labels for the mailer or envelope. A third option is to invest in a few rubber stamps. Possibilities for rubber stamps are:

1. Return address (include phone number).
2. "CLASS OF ___ REUNION INFORMATION ENCLOSED"
3. "ADDRESS CORRECTION REQUESTED" (Explained on p. 60.)
4. "FIRST CLASS MAIL"
5. School logo or mascot (by special order).

These stamps can all be used with bright colored inks (school colors?) for emphasis and decorative effect.

Return address labels are anywhere from about $3 per 1000 for gummed to about $4 per 250 for self-stick. They may take 4 to 8 weeks to get, though, so order early. (See Appendix A, Walter Drake and Sons.) There are places in larger towns and cities where you can get rubber stamps the same day you place the order. They run $8 to $15 each, plus the pad and extra ink. Self-inking stamps run $12 to $18 each. Number ten (long) envelopes with your return address printed in the upper left hand corner run about $35 per 1000 (minimum order) and take 3 to 4 weeks. (See Appendix A, Quill Corp.) Imprinted envelopes also come in quantities of 100. (See Appendix A, Walter Drake and Sons.)

Postage

Each of your mailers will probably weigh less than 3 ounces. And since Third Class costs the same as First Class up to that weight, plan on mailing everything First Class. We don't recommend a bulk mailing permit (Third Class mail). For one thing, it costs $100 (1989) just to get the permit: $50 per year plus $50 to register. For another, your mailers may not be delivered for up to 3 to 4 weeks after you mail them. Third Class mail also requires that you sort it by zip code, bundle it, put special stickers on each bundle, weigh it, fill out special forms, and take it to the Post Office (and only the Post Office that issued the permit). Taking both the money and time into account, it seems wiser to stick with First Class. Also, First Class is automatically forwarded by the Post Office and Third Class is not.

Domestic First Class postage rates and Mexico (1989):
> 25 cents for one ounce
> 45 cents for two ounces
> 15 cents per postcard

First Class postage rates to Canada (1989):
> 30 cents for one ounce
> 52 cents for two ounces
> 21 cents per postcard

When sending mail to a person in the military overseas, regular domestic rates apply if you use an A.P.O. or F.P.O. address.

Using standard sized paper (8½ × 11):
Five sheets plus one regular envelope will go for one ounce.
Four sheets plus one long envelope will go for one ounce.
Ten sheets plus one long envelope will go for two ounces.

Using legal sized paper (8½ × 14):
Three sheets plus one long envelope will go for one ounce.
Eight sheets plus one long envelope will go for two ounces.

Desktop Publishing

If someone in your group has a computer/software combination that is capable of desktop publishing, or if someone has the knowledge of how to use one (through job experience, for example), then you can come up with some truly impressive mailers or newsletters for not much money.

Amazing things can be done on personal computers these days. To find out exactly what, ask for a demonstration of desktop publishing at one of your local computer stores. The most "user friendly" computer is probably the MacIntosh. One of the least expensive is the Atari ST. Newsletters and mailers can be created with dot matrix printers, but laser printers produce much higher quality. The good news is that you don't have to own the laser printer (since they cost an arm and a leg). IF you get the right software, you can take your disk (or mail it) to a place that will output on a laser printer for you for about $1–2 per page. **These pages are then your originals from which photocopies or quick-print copies are made.** Some of these places also rent computers by the hour (you work at the store), but you have to know how to use the software or else you will be wasting your time and money. Some of the fancier copy or print shops around universities are set up with such services, otherwise ask at a local computer store.

The Survey (See Figure 17)

A survey of your classmates can be an interesting and useful item to include in your mailers, but there is no use in going to the extra trouble unless you know for sure that you will compile and use the results. Here are some ways that a survey can be used:

1. To provide information for some of the awards to be presented during the reunion program. Decide on the award categories first, then formulate the questions that will provide the answers. In most cases it is more appropriate to ask for the following type of response: "If any of you think you may qualify for any of these awards, please let us know: Most Recent Parent, Newest Grandparent, First to Retire, Married the Most." Of course, you should still not judge the winner solely by the responses received. Some people will not bother to send back the survey, or feel too self-conscious to do so. A few discrete questions may have to be asked before the awards are presented, and as a last resort, right before each winner is announced, ask if anyone can claim to better the record in question. See the end of Chapter 10 for a list of award categories and suggestions.

2. To compile biographical information for a class directory, a newspaper, a memory book, or a collection of short biographies. The minimal information is: name, address, phone number, and spouse's name (for the name tags). The next level of involvement could include: birthdate, children's names and ages, number of grandchildren (if any), occupation(s), and hobbies. Beyond that are: highlights of your life (or of the last 10 years, or since the last reunion); favorite quote, saying, or proverb; favorite books, movies, or music; and pet peeve.

3. To collect information that can be used later for a "re-find" if the person gets "lost" again. In this category are: birthdate, social security number, service number, driver's license number, and address of "someone who will always know where you are." The more serious groups (such as family and military associations) are the ones who usually gather this type of information. When doing so, be up front about it and explain your purpose.

4. For a chart of "Class Statistics" to be displayed at the reunion. The information can also be a part of the memory book, or included in anything that is mailed out after the reunion. This statistical "class portrait" can include the following:

• Total number in class.

• Number of men.

- Number of women.
- How many live outside U.S.
- Percentage who still live within 50 miles of school.
- Total number of states represented by class.
- How many (or what percentage) married.
- Total number (or percentage) never married.
- Total number of children born to classmates.
- Total number of grandchildren.
- Number of classmates that can't be "found."
- Number (or percentage) that attended the reunion.
- How many deceased.

Encourage all your classmates to fill out and return the survey, even if they can't attend the reunion. And have survey forms at the reunion for those who did not send them in.

```
                        CLASS SURVEY
               Lakeside High School Class of '69
                   Return Deadline: July 1

        The information that you provide here will appear in our
    class directory which will be printed in the memory book and
    mailed out after the reunion. If you attend the reunion, there
    is no additional charge for the memory book. If you can't attend
    the reunion, the memory book can be purchased for $7, postpaid.

    Full Name _____

    Address _____

    City _____ State _____ Zip _____

    Phone ( _____ ) _____

    Spouse's name _____

    _____Sorry, I can't attend. Please send me a memory book. Enclosed
    is $7 made out to: "Lakeside Class of '69".

    Return to:  Mary Smith Jamison
                1234 Main St.
                Anytown, CA 94444
                415/555-6666

    REMEMBER: The return deadline is July 1.
```

FIGURE 17. *The above survey is for absolute minimal information. The next step up is to ask for more biographical information (see #2, p. 102). Or you can go all out and ask for information for awards, re-finds, and/or statistics (see #1, #3, and #4, p.102).*

REGISTRATION: Save $5 PER PERSON by paying before April 1.

$27 per person BEFORE April 1.
$32 per person AFTER April 1.
Final deadline: July 1.

Reservations are important! NO TICKETS WILL BE SOLD AT THE DOOR!

WHERE?   Fort Washington Country Club
              1700 Fort Washington Dr.
              Fresno, CA 93207
              (209) 555-7766

WHEN?   Saturday, July 22, 1989
              6 p.m. to 2 a.m.

DRESS?   Casual to semi-formal

___Yes, I will be there.
___Sorry, I can't attend.

Name _____
        First   (Maiden) *   Last

Phone (_____)_____

Number attending _____   Amount enclosed $_____

My guest's name tag should read: _____
                                    First   Last

Do we have your correct address? _____ If not, please write your
correct address on the back of this form.

Make checks payable to: "Sanger High 1961 Reunion"

No tickets will be sent. The receipt of your check guarantees
your tickets at the door.

Send your check and the survey form to:

              Mary Smith
              223 S. Main St.
              Sanger, CA 93657
              (209) 555-1234

FIGURE 18. Here is an example of a Registration Form to be included with the mailer. You may decide on a different tactic, for example: ask for a $10 deposit, or offer a $5 discount to anyone who sends in a $20 deposit before a certain date. The important thing is to get the money coming in one way or another.

CHAPTER 9

Getting Ready

*The Facility – Decorations – Imprinted Napkins – Name Tags –
Photos/Memory Book – Video – Mementos/Imprinted Giftware –
Music – Choosing a Band – Disc Jockeys – Doing Without – Taped
Music – Activity Centers – Refreshments – Slides/Movies/Old
Photos – Residence Map – Bulletin Board/Memorabilia Table – In
Memorium.*

The Facility

It's a good idea to look into all aspects of using the facility **ahead
of time.** Of course, with commercial facilities, large or small, there
should be someone there during the entire event who is familiar
with the building. However, if you are renting a Grange Hall,
church social room, community center, or similar facility, this may
not be the case. Quite often someone will open up and close up, but
will not be there in between (be sure to get this person's home
phone number before he or she leaves). If so, do you know how to
take care of blown fuses, where the heating and air-conditioning
controls are, how to locate the various light and electrical switches?
Are the restrooms, coat rooms, and storage rooms unlocked? Are
there materials for cleaning up spilled drinks, food, broken glass? Is
your group expected to clean up after itself? When? That night or
the next day? People in charge of clean-up should be assigned far in
advance so they can plan to stay late or come early the following
day. Are there brooms, dust pans, garbage cans, garbage can liners,
etc.? Are all the financial aspects of using the facility taken care of?
If not, take your reunion account check book with you the evening
of the event. A week or two before the event confirm (again) your
date and time with the manager.

A public address system (PA system) helps tremendously for any event of more than about 25 people. Remember: People at reunions are more excited and have shorter attention spans than people at other types of events. It's virtually impossible to conduct a program or make an announcement without a sound system. Most facilities have their own PA systems. If not, consider borrowing or renting one. If you are hiring a band or DJ, get permission **in advance** to use their sound system for your program and announcements.

A podium adds a sense of professionalism to the program. Borrow or rent one, if at all possible. DJ's often set up their own podium at reunions, but you should not necessarily assume that it can be used for your purposes. These podiums are set up in the dance area before the reunion starts and are usually full of electronic equipment which makes them hard to move. If the dance area is in a different location from the program area, you should plan on having your own separate podium. Ask the DJ. He or she may have an extra, or should know where one could be borrowed or rented.

Be sure the room or hall you are renting has enough electrical outlets and the wattage to accommodate your needs: sound system, slide and movie projectors, tape recorders, bands with electrical instruments, and photographers with special lighting needs. Are extension cords needed? Duct tape (available at any hardware store) is best for taping extension cords to the floor or carpet so that people won't trip over them. How about chairs and extra tables for snacks, memorabilia, and registration?

You may want to ask the manager about the facility's security arrangements. Is there a safe place to store coats and bags? If rain is a possibility, is there a place for raincoats and umbrellas? Check whether there is on-site or nearby parking available. Nothing can be more frustrating than spending half the evening looking for a parking space. Most facilities are accessible to the handicapped, but it's always wise to double check on this if it's needed.

If the facility prohibits smoking, you may want to consider some areas where smokers can congregate. Conversely, if the facility allows smoking, consider providing a no-smoking room or a group of tables during dinner for non-smokers. Post several signs that explain the smoking/no-smoking policy.

A day or two before the reunion, many facilities will require that you guarantee a certain number of meals (to be paid for the evening of the reunion). The reason for this is so that the kitchen knows how much food to order and prepare. You should have a fairly good idea of the meal count by then, but there is no way that you can come up with an exact number (and the manager realizes this, too). The important thing is to NEVER guarantee more than you have money to pay for (or more than you can GET money to pay for). If you have 150 people signed up and paid for, it is realistic to want to guarantee 170 meals. But if you don't have the money in your account, you had better find a donor or plan on a raffle or some other way of coming up with the money.

Decorations

Decorations are always nice but never necessary at reunions. The first consideration is whether your group has someone with talent, interest, and the ability to recruit and motivate helpers. Next, consider the cost and be careful when budgeting. Decorations are no longer the nickle and dime items they were years ago. If you have the interest and expertise on your committee for an extensive decoration job, then be sure to write out a carefully itemized list of materials ahead of time. Then price out each item and total it up. An "all-out" decoration job with flowers on each table, banners, crepe paper streamers, imprinted balloons and napkins, etc., can easily run $300–400 and we have seen as high as $700.

But first find out the facility's rules about decorating. Some places don't allow thumb tacks or tape. Others will allow tape but no thumb tacks. Such rules may limit you to table centerpieces and banners. Can the facility be decorated ahead of time, and if so, when can you have access to the building? School gyms, Grange Halls, and community centers can sometimes be decorated a day or two ahead, but banquet halls, if they can be decorated at all, are usually available only a few hours ahead. This may put a real limit on your decorating plans. Also, consider how much help you will need. One or two very talented people may still not be able to do a good job in only two hours. And if your plans are too elaborate, even a crew of 6 or 8 could be too exhausted to enjoy the event. Remember, the decorators will want to go home to clean up and change (and rest!).

But remember that a reunion is not a masquerade ball or even the Senior Prom. You can keep decorations simple, tasteful, and relatively inexpensive, and still maintain the spirit of the reunion. Try to incorporate school colors into balloons, simple flower arrangements, place settings and tablecloths. Here are some suggestions:

For table centerpieces, balloons are probably the cheapest way to go these days. In larger metropolitan areas you can have helium balloon bouquets delivered, or you can rent the helium tanks and inflate them yourself. Estimate the number of tables and figure three to six latex balloons with one mylar (foil) balloon in the middle for a nice looking centerpiece. You can write or draw on the foil balloon (easiest when not inflated) in colored ink using marking pens. The super-large markers work best for this. You can use colored gift wrapping ribbon for "string," or the flashy metallic mylar ribbon available in party supply stores. The balloons can be tied to a decorative weighted object that is placed in the center of the table. Be careful to not make this weighted object (the part that rests on the table) too large, since during the meal you may need all the room you can get for the food and utensils. The helium balloons themselves will rise up out of the way and present no problem. See Figure 19A.

Floral arrangements are also popular for centerpieces, but are a bit more expensive than balloons. However, bud vases with just a few bright flowers are attractive and cheaper. Flowers can also double as door prizes. If you know someone with a large flower garden or someone in the floral business, you might get free or discounted flowers, or at least an experienced flower arranger or advisor. A local florist may be interested in giving you a discount in exchange for free advertisement such as a sign at the reunion or a card at each table reading: "Flower Arrangements Donated by (florist's name)".

A dessert cake, just big enough to feed the people at each table, makes a nice centerpiece. Of course, school colors and appropriate words and mascots can be used in decorating the cake. Numbers and letters made of sugar can be bought at dime stores, drug stores, or supermarkets.

Pennants and banners can be made from butcher paper and poster paint. These can be embellished by using crepe paper and glued-on stars or glitter, all of which come in many colors. Your school may be willing to loan you some banners and pennants, especially for a small donation. If you are having a group photo taken, a banner can

FIGURE 19A. Helium balloons (foil and/or latex) make a nice table center-piece. The foil can be written on with large marking pens (easier before inflating).

FIGURE 19B. An aging mascot greeted members of Hudson's Bay High School, Vancouver, WA. A small version could be used in newsletters or imprinted memorabilia.

also serve for identification purposes. It can read: "(name of school), Class of 19..." Silver 25's or gold 50's are nice if one of these numbers is the year of your reunion. These numbers in metal foil, glitter, or spray paint can appear very large at the entrance to the reunion or behind a speaker's podium. Or they can be made much smaller and be part of the centerpieces on each table.

A sign maker or cartoonist may be able to make a sign for you like the one in Figure 19B. It depicts an aging school mascot greeting classmates as they come in the door. For such a purpose the size should be at least 2' × 3' or even larger, but a cartoon for your mailers or newsletter would also be nice.

But remember: What goes up must come down. Make careful plans for the removal of the decorations. Some facilities will charge a deposit or clean-up fee just in case no one shows to clean up. Assign this job to your most responsible and sincere helpers.

Visit a party supply store to get more ideas. In the Yellow Pages see: "Balloons, Novelty and Toy, Retail," "Party Equipment, Renting," and "Party Supplies."

Imprinted Napkins. Napkins and coasters in school colors and imprinted with the school emblem or mascot can add a classy touch to your reunion. You can see samples and order these from most stores that sell wedding, graduation, or prom items and supplies. Also try greeting card stores. If you can't find a store near you, call Carlson Craft at (507) 625-5011 and ask for the customer service department. Carlson is one of the wholesalers that supply many small stores around the country, but they do not sell directly to the consumer. Ask for their representative nearest you who has a Graduation Album or an All Occasion Album. These albums have the school mascots, type styles, and colors that you will be looking for. Some stores have only the Wedding Album, which for you is a waste of time. Carlson's hours are: 7am to 7pm, M–F and 7:30am to 3pm on Saturday (Central Time).

Name Tags

Inability to recognize old friends or remember names is one of the most common fears reported by reunion-goers. A name tag consisting of a copy of the senior picture along with the person's name in large letters will take care of this problem. Put the same senior picture on the spouse's (or guest's) tag along with the spouse's (or guest's) name. Then people will have an easier time figuring out who is with whom. This will make the evening more pleasant for the spouses or guests, too, since it will eliminate people staring at them trying to figure out if they are a member of the class.

A good copy machine can do a fairly decent job of reproducing photographs for name tags, and is certainly cheaper than any other method. But it's important to compare samples (the Xerox brand copiers seem to do the best job on photographs) and contrasts (most machines have a contrast adjustment). Most class photos must be increased in size for name tag purposes. With many photocopy machines this is very easy to do and the clerk will usually help you determine the amount of increase. But if you must figure it yourself, it's really not too difficult. An increase or a decrease in size is expressed as a percentage. 100% equals no change in size. An increase in size (enlargement) is more than 100%, and a decrease in size (reduction) is less than 100%. Measure one side of your original photograph. Then divide that number into the length of the same side after it has been enlarged to the size you want. For example, if your original photo is 2 inches high, and you want to enlarge it to 3 inches, then divide 2 into 3 and multiply by 100. The result is 150%. Some machines will increase by this amount and some won't. Check around by phone first.

Make two copies of all the senior pictures in the yearbook—do a whole page at a time. You will need two copies so you can make name tags for the spouses. By the way, enlargements cost more than regular copies. So instead of making two enlargements, try making one enlargement and then a regular copy of the enlargement. Some quality will be compromised because you are making a copy of a copy. But some machines are capable of usable results by this method. At least it's worth a try. If you don't like the results, get two enlargements.

The copies can be made onto regular white paper or onto solid self-adhesive peel-off paper. ("Solid" meaning no scored divisions as with address labels — you must furnish this paper, available at stationery stores). Cut out the copied photos and rubber-cement them (if they are on regular paper) or stick them (if they are on self-adhesive paper) onto large labels, file cards, or construction paper. With colored ink, ribbons, and more construction paper, you can make the name tags festive looking and incorporate the school colors. Be sure you leave enough room at the bottom or side of the label to write the person's name. Make the letters large and clear enough so that people won't have to squint or get up too close to the name tag to read it. Buy a large felt-tip pen for this purpose and find someone who can print well. (Letters ¼" high should be the minimum size, ⅜" is better.) Be sure to emphasize the maiden names of the women by either underlining or printing them in all capital letters. Make name tags in advance for everyone who is coming. You will also want to take all the necessary items for making name tags to the reunion and assign someone to make them on the spot for last minute drop-ins, or re-make any that weren't done correctly. If you have peel-off, self sticking name tags, then also have pins available for those who would rather not stick the tags onto their clothing.

"Button" name tags look nice and make nice souvenirs, but the standard size (2¼") is too small to be easily read. The minimum size for a button name tag is 2¾" in diameter which can be very expensive. The name-of-the-game with name tags is not just "identification" but "EASY identification." Luckily, the method that gives you the best results (making them by hand) is also the cheapest. See Figures 20A and 20B.

The tags can be put out in alphabetical order on the registration table, or for smaller reunions they can be placed out randomly for people to pick up as they arrive. If there is a matter that needs to be discussed with someone (such as payment), set that person's name tag aside or attach a note to it.

Name tags can also be used for control purposes. For example, if you see someone without a name tag, you know they have not yet been to the registration table. Or, if some people are to be present but not eat the meal (this would have to be pre-arranged with the facility), a colored dot on the name tag could indicate to the waiters that the person is not to be served.

NEVER let people make their own name tags, even though it's a time-saver. You will get a lot of tags that you can't read, or people identified only as "Al" or "Linda."

Photo name tags may not be necessary for small groups where everyone knows each other or for younger groups just a few years out of school. But even with these groups, such name tags are appreciated by the spouses and guests. If you decide not to have photo name tags, it's still helpful and relatively easy to distinguish classmates from spouses, guests, or teachers:

1. Classmates could have a special button or badge reading "Alumni of (name of school)," "Class of ___," etc.

2. Guests could have a button, name tag, or ribbon reading "Guest," or "Quit staring, I'm a guest." (See Figure 21.)

FIGURE 20A. These are examples of standard sized name tags. As seen here on the printed page, they seem large enough, but both are too small to be easily read in a real situation.

All this may seem like a lot of work, but attention to details like these will go a long way to making your reunion comfortable and fun for everyone. Just knowing they will be able to recognize former classmates — and that they themselves will be recognized — will help put people at ease. You should mention this plan for making name tags in your mailers. That way people won't be so apprehensive about the recognition problem, and more will attend.

FIGURE 20B. A rectangle is a more efficient shape for a name tag than a circle. This example is the same size as a standard 3 × 5 card. The photo can be easily seen and the name easily read. No need to bend over and squint.

QUIT STARING!

I did **NOT** graduate with you.

(I am a guest)

name _____

FIGURE 21. Everyone at a reunion should have a name tag. A person who is not a classmate, the spouse or date of a classmate, or a teacher could wear a name tag like this. This would include anyone who is working at the reunion, an observer from another reunion committee, etc. This name tag may be photocopied. Transpose your preference of image.

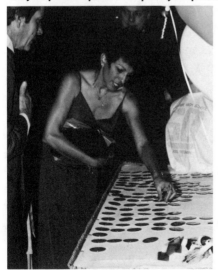

Having classmates choose their name tags, instead of handing them out, gives people something interesting to do.

There was no problem with recognition at this grade school reunion. The name tags were made on 5 × 8 cards and hung around the neck. Glencoe Public School, Glencoe, IL, Class of '31, 50th reunion. Photographer: James Ferry.

Photos/Memory Book (also see p. 137)

Three kinds of photos can be taken at reunions:

1. The class group photo.
2. Individual color portraits (combined with memory book) taken with spouse or date.
3. Candid photos.

There are photographers who specialize in taking pictures of groups, classes, reunions and so on. Some will offer the color-portrait/memory-book package only. Others will only take group photos. Others will do either. Look in the Yellow Pages under "Photographers." Since most photographers don't offer this service, phone one and ask who does, or phone any school and ask who takes their class and yearbook photos. Chances are the same company will take reunion photos. If not, they (the yearbook photographer) will know for sure who does. Prices and quality vary, so ask to see samples of the photographer's work. If you can get a recommendation from another reunion group, so much the better. Other reunion groups can sometimes be contacted through your school office.

Group photos are the most common type at small reunions (under 100 people in the photo). They should be taken by a professional because indoor settings present lighting problems few amateurs can overcome. Usually spouses are not included in group photos, but teachers are. If your group is over 100 (don't count spouses), it may be too large to organize and control, and faces will appear too small. (For a solution to this latter problem, you might consider a larger format photo, say 11 × 18. Of course, this will cost more.) The worst thing about a group photo is that faces may be hidden behind other faces. This is because people think that if they can see the camera, then their entire face will appear in the photo, and this isn't necessarily the case. It takes a lot of time and an experienced photographer to arrange everyone properly.

An 8 × 10 color print should cost from $5 to $8 per person. It works best to include the cost of the photo into the total cost of the

The photographer needs room to work. Set aside an area. He or she will arrive early to set up.

event (rather than charging separately for the photo). Also offer the photo to those who can't attend. Have a special place on the registration form for this, and don't forget to add the mailing cost to the price.

At most reunions, professional photographers take **color portraits** of each individual along with their spouse or date, similar to the ones we may remember from our high school proms. And like the prom photos, this usually requires waiting in line. Also there will be a photographer's card to fill out that serves the dual purpose of connecting the right name with the photo (for the memory book), and providing an address to which the portraits and the memory book will be sent. These portraits are offered for purchase through the mail about 6 to 8 weeks after the reunion. They are almost always mailed out on a trial basis, that is: the person is at no obligation to buy.

Along with the portraits, a **memory book** (sometimes called a mini-yearbook) is included which the reunion committee has already paid for. The original photos are taken in color but are usually printed in black-and-white in the memory book. However, new technology is making "color photo" memory books more reasonable in price. In 1989 the average was $6 for black-and-white and $10 for color. This differential will probably decrease even more in the next few years.

In addition to individual photos of those who attend the reunion, memory books can contain (see Figures 22 A–C):

1. a class directory with addresses of all the classmates (and sometimes a short biography).

2. an introduction and acknowledgement page.

3. a statement from the committee.

4. a photo of the committee.

5. a montage page of candid photos taken at the reunion.

6. a memorial page.

These additions must be created (typed and pasted up) by the reunion committee, or more explicitly: by the individual assigned by the committee. (Examples and instructions are provided by the company.) The memory book is paid for as part of the reunion fee; those who did not attend can buy one through the mail. Typical

Held at the   10 Year Class Reunion
National Orange Show Restaurant   May 24, 1980
P.O. BOX 2426, SAN BERNARDINO, CALIFORNIA 92406
TELEPHONE 889-6159

PACIFIC HIGH SCHOOL
Class of '70

Hi Alumni! Our ten year class reunion has come and gone. To all of us who attended, it'll be an evening we will long remember.

It was great seeing all those faces from the past and rediscovering old friendships. What a strange, but nice feeling to talk to a mature adult, while vividly remembering that seventeen year old kid he or she used to be.

We regret that some of our classmates were unable to attend, but we hope everyone will be at our fifteenth year reunion to be held in 1985. To make it easier to locate people for that reunion, please keep us up to date on your current address. Send your change of address to Diane Rousseau Coronado (address listed in back of booklet) or contact Pacific High School in 1985. Your reunion committee is already making tentative plans for the next reunion. If you have any ideas or want to be on the committee, please drop us a line.

A big thanks to all of you who attended. YOU made the evening a real success. A special thanks to Gary St. Germain's band, "Paradox". Hope we will be seeing you all in 1985 and best wishes for the coming five years.

Your Committee,

Diane Rousseau Coronado
Vicki Rudh-Wilson
Babette DeJean Butterfield
Rita Garcia Carlos
Jenny Arellano De La Torre
Irma Genera Romero
Alfred Romero
Paul Garrity
Johnetta Hanna Davis
Carey Davis

P. S. If you would be interested in attending the homecoming game this fall, please send a self-addressed stamped envelope for more information.

FIGURE 22A. The memory book offers the committee a chance to address the whole class. But this will appear only if you take the time to write it and send it in.

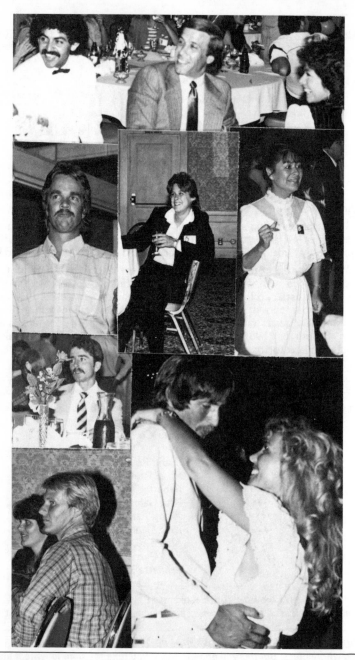

FIGURE 22B. A Montage Page of candid photos taken at the reunion can
be a part of your memory book.

Directory

ACOSTA, David - 3149 Del Rey Dr., San Bernardino, CA	92404
ACOSTA, Dennis - 3149 Del Rey Dr., San Bernardino, CA	92404
ADAMSON, Gayle - 764 E. 23rd St., San Bernardino, CA	92404
ALBA, Barbara - 17673 Randall, Fontana, CA	
ALBIDREZ, Tony - P.O. Box 754, Colorado CD, TX	79512
ALLRED, Jacki - 1912 Harding Rd., S. Aberdeen, WA	98520
ALVARADO, Arthur - 140 Auburn Ct., Redlands, CA	92373
ALVARADO, Joe & Janice - 1847-D Wheatloop, Apt. D, Yuma, AZ	85364
ALVARADO, Yolanda - 1053 Magnolia St., San Bernardino, CA	
ALVAREZ,David - 1232 Edgar Ave., Beaumont, CA	92223
ALVAREZ, Patsy - 1053 W. 7th St., San Bernardino, CA	92411
(ALVAREZ), Yolanda Reyna - 7172 Glasgow, San Bernardino, CA	92404
AMBERG, Jim - 8941 Brooke, Westminster, CA	92683
AMPARAN, Mario - c/o 2217 2nd Ave., San Bernardino, CA	92405
(ANDREWS), Pat & Moon Cloud - Box 3102, Kodiak, AK	99603
ANWAY, Jeff - 2744 N. Fremontia Dr., San Bernardino, CA	92404
ARCE, Betty - 3005 Loma Ave., San Bernardino, CA	92404
(ARELLANO), Jenny & Tony De La Torre - 1471 Valencia, San Bernardino, CA	92404
ARMENTA, Mark - 4078 Cajon Blvd., San Bernardino, CA	
(ARRANTS), Rosann & Chris Moulis - 726 Daffodil Way, Concord, CA	94518
ARROLLO, Betty - 741 N. Arrowhead Ave., San Bernardino, CA	
(ARTOFF), Debbie & Tom Thompson - 7429 W. Evans Creek Rd., Rogue River, OR	97537
(ASKELAND), Susan & Richard Rizzoli - 5390 Palm Grove Ct., San Jose, CA	95123
ATHANASSOPOULAS, Helen - 105 N. "J" St., San Bernardino, CA	92410
ATMORE, Robert & Deborah- PSC Box 609, APO San Francisco, CA	96328
AVILA, Maria - 1920 Pico St., San Bernardino, CA	
BAILEY, Ken - Route 1, Box 3039 Warrenton, OR	97146
(BAKER), Linda Pecchia - 3580 Main St., Riverside, CA	92501
BALLARD, David - 2406 S. Pacific, Boise, ID	83705
(BARBER), Vikki & Pat Rogers - 804 W. Sequoia, San Bernardino, CA	92407
(BARKER), Susan Howie - 1381 W. Rialto Ave., San Bernardino, CA	92410
(BARNETT), Ruth & David Hollenbeck - 405 Smithridge Park, Reno, NV	89502
BAUMAN, Cyndie - 3724 Spencer Apt. 322, Torrance, CA	90503

FIGURE 22C. Most memory books contain a directory (above). The memory book company usually offers a scroll (or equivalent) for a Memorial Page (below).

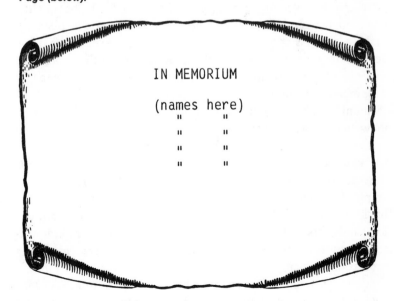

IN MEMORIUM

(names here)
"   "

"   "

"   "

"   "

charges for memory books are: 100 minimum at $8 each; at around 400 the price goes down to about $6 each. These books are by far the most popular form of souvenir created for reunions.

Candid photos taken with a Polaroid camera are a lot of fun at reunions. Almost always they are done by one or more members (or friends) of the group. Professionals can't make enough profit to offer this service. Since Polaroid film is rather expensive, your volunteer photographer may want to charge for the cost of the film on a per-photo basis, paid for at the time the picture is taken (usually $2–3). These Polaroid shots can also appear in the memory book on the photo montage page, if you choose to have one. If a photo is to be printed, black-and-white always works best. If your photographer is also creating a memory book, he or she may take candid non-Polaroid photos for the photo montage page, if you ask. There may be an additional charge for this. You might also consider having candid photos taken for a reunion scrapbook, which can be brought out and added to at each successive reunion. After three or four reunions, such a scrapbook would have quite a story to tell.

Video

Commercial video tapes of reunions are becoming increasingly popular as video equipment becomes cheaper and of higher quality. Over 50 percent of American households own video playback machines, and that percentage will only increase over the next few years. But so far, video is being employed along with, rather than instead of, photography and memory books as a means of documenting reunions.

Reunion videos contain two types of footage. One is the "interview" where each person is asked questions and he or she replies on camera. The other is "candid shots" where the cameraman wanders through the reunion taking footage of people talking, dancing, eating, etc. These are then edited together and background music and graphics are added. In some cases "shots" of old photos and yearbooks are also added. The final product is usually 60–120 minutes long and costs $20–30 per tape. Additional footage of the committee in action, decorating for the reunion, and next-day picnics add a professional touch, but cost extra.

Some video companies charge a base fee plus so much per tape sold. Others do not charge a base fee, but must be guaranteed a

The videographer will roam through the crowd (above), as well as interview people at a station under lights (below). Shown is Richard Raines of Rich's Video Service, Martinez, CA.

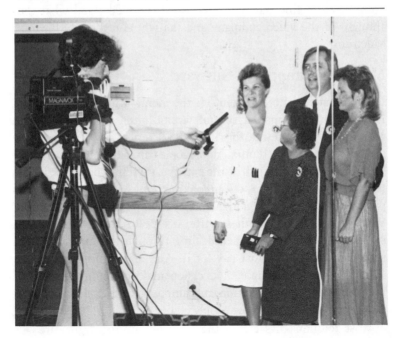

minimum purchase. In the latter case, the committee or the company advertises the tape through the mail beforehand. If not enough tapes are pre-sold, then the video services are cancelled. By the way, a sales point for video is that you do not need to own a VCR to enjoy a reunion video. VCR's are extremely cheap to rent for one evening. All you need is a TV.

In some cases, video at reunions is done on a completely freelance basis. There is no charge to the reunion committee, and the sale of the product is done through the mail. Arrangements of this kind often involve people who are trying to break into the field. This doesn't necessarily mean that quality will be compromised, but it does mean that you should be careful. Even though the video service is not costing you anything, your classmates will expect a high quality product, and you are the one in charge of the selection process. The quality of a video tape depends on the skill of the person operating the camera, the skill of the editor, and the skill of the interviewer. (For low-budget assignments this may be the same person.) It's very important to preview a reunion video that the company has already produced. Then call someone on that reunion committee to find out how they liked the video, and what they thought of the video company and the whole process of having a video done.

Mementos/Imprinted Giftware

The most common memento is the memory book, but the problem is that it is mailed several weeks (often months) after the reunion is over. Likewise for videos. It's a very classy gesture to give out something at the reunion that people can take home with them. If the item is of high quality, the extra cost will not be noticed. This is an important point: A cheap looking item will draw complaints ("waste of money"), but a high quality item will gain compliments. When choosing one of these gifts, it's VERY important to see a sample ahead of time. When dealing through the mail, ask for a sample even if you must pay for it. And allow enough time for: 1. mailing of the sample, 2. decision making among committee members, and 3. preparation and shipping of the order. This all takes a lot longer than most people realize.

Most reunion gifts are in the form of imprinted giftware — a keepsake that will last through the years as a souvenir and remembrance of the reunion. They usually cost somewhere between $2 and $8, and can also be used as "fund-raisers" by selling them for a dollar or two more than they cost. It's best to have your classmates pay for their mementos by including the cost into the admission price, rather than by taking orders and charging separately. Of course, those who can't attend the reunion should be able to order their's separately, but for the others, plan on one memento for each

person attending. Examples of imprinted gifts are: marble paperweights, felt pennants, coasters, key rings, wine glasses, coffee mugs, decks of playing cards, bumperstickers and T-shirts.

T-shirts are popular mementoes, but you must be careful not to over-buy. The number "60" on this T-shirt is made up of the names of the graduates. Woodside High School, Woodside, CA.

Music

Choosing a Band. The two key questions here are: What kind of music do you want, and how much do you want to spend? Discuss these with the committee first, then start asking around. Perhaps you can get a recommendation from another reunion committee. If you have friends or former classmates who play in bands, be very careful and tactful. The quality, style, or price may not be at all what you want. Try to find out how long the band has played together and whether it has bookings weeks or even months in advance. The reason for this is that musical groups are notoriously unstable or short-lived. They have even been known to break up without notifying anyone. Also, be sure to ask if the band can play music dating from your high school years. After you have narrowed the field down, **if at all possible, listen to the groups at a live engagement,** rather than on records or tapes, before you make your decision. Most bands require a deposit and a contract, and be sure to re-confirm the engagement two or three weeks before the reunion. The rates vary widely for bands, from $200–300 for an inexperienced 3-person group to $1000 and more for a large, established group. The average at reunions is $400–500. Check the Yellow Pages under "Entertainers," "Musicians," or "Orchestras and Bands"; in the white pages look up "Musicians' Union." The companies who manage bands and DJ's are called booking agents, and can be found under "Entertainment Bureaus," or "Professional Talent Management."

Disc jockeys (DJ's) are becoming very popular with reunion organizers. A good DJ has a tape collection of thousands of songs, amazingly sophisticated equipment, and will be able to play music from almost any era and also take requests. Most of them have lists of the top ten songs for any month and year, and a reference system that allows them to find, cue up, and play any request in a matter of seconds. And it's a lot easier to tell a DJ to "keep it down" than a band. The best thing is that you get to hear the exact rendition of the song you remember, rather than a band's interpretation. For nostalgia purposes, this can be important.

There are people in almost every community who hire out as disc jockeys for events such as reunions and parties. Their rates vary between $300 and $500 per event. Rates below $200 should be viewed with some skepticism as to what you are actually getting. We strongly urge that you try to "review" a DJ in action before making a selection. And remember that you are not necessarily looking for Mr. Personality. You don't want entertainment at a reunion. Some DJ's actually don't like to do reunions because they can't let their personality "shine through." What you need is someone with a good selection of the music you are looking for, sophisticated equipment that allows him or her to find your requests easily, and who is helpful and understanding of the needs of a reunion. An experienced DJ will help make suggestions for your program, and be supportive of those participants with stage fright. (In most cases, you can use the DJ's sound system and maybe the podium for your program.) Some of the local radio DJ's may provide this service, but these are usually the "personality" types. Look in the Yellow Pages under "Entertainers." (Also see where to find booking agents under "Choosing a Band," above.)

The Disc Jockey should not be "the life of the party" at a reunion. A good DJ with "reunion experience" knows how to stay in the background, and can offer professional advice and encouragement to the people involved with the program. Don Fitzsimmons of Antioch, CA (top), and Carl Mindling of San Jose, CA.

Doing Without. If you must eliminate one major expense, we recommend that you do without "live" music or a DJ, and instead have your own taped music or records. (See p. 39, "Ways to Save Money.")

Taped Music. Before dinner while people are socializing, taped music provides a nice background, **but don't play it too loud.** It should be music with significance to the class, such as songs that were popular at the time of graduation. Very few commercial records or tapes can give you the variety you will want, so try to tape selections from a private collection. You may find people who are willing to do this by mentioning it in the mailers. Almost every class has one or two people who have kept their high school record collection over the years. Cassettes will work fine; higher quality reel-to-reel tape is not necessary. Records are best, however, because they make it easier to play requests (tapes being more difficult to cue up).

Background music can be played on any home stereo system. However, the volume will need to be louder for dance music, and a small home stereo system may not have enough wattage (power) if the room is large. The only way to test this is to take the stereo to the room and try it, but even this is tricky because in a real situation you have "crowd noise" to contend with. "Auditorium sized" amplifiers and speakers can be rented, at least in the larger metropolitan areas, and some DJ's offer a "sound system only" for considerably less cost than their usual package. Be sure you also have someone available that evening to change tapes or records, and keep an eye on the equipment. An extension cord may be necessary. Know where the fuses or breaker boxes are. Tape electrical cords to the floor or rug with duct tape.

Activity Centers

Remember, your main concern is to make everyone comfortable. Activity centers — old photos, movies, slides, memorabilia table, bulletin boards, residence map, refreshment table, memorial display, etc.—allow people to mingle naturally. These focal points will also give them something to talk about besides the weather or their kids. Be sure to explain this concept to your volunteers so they can understand "why," as well as "what," they are doing.

Refreshments. Many people in social situations need something to do with their hands and their mouths (other than talk) in order to feel at ease. Unfortunately, alcohol often fills this role. Some people will drink more than they want to, especially if liquor is the only thing available. Having chips and dip, nuts, fruit juice, coffee and other refreshments and "finger food" available throughout the evening gives people more options and helps cushion the effects of the alcohol. Assign volunteers to replenish these snacks.

And for dessert they ate their school — presented here in the form of a cake. Nevada City High School, Nevada City, CA. Year of reunion and photographer unknown. The school has been torn down.

Slides/Movies/Old Photos. Everyone enjoys looking at their past. You can set aside a corner equipped with a slide projector, a screen, and a table or bulletin board with old photos (grammar school photos are great fun, too). You should also consider keeping a scrapbook of each reunion. These will become more and more interesting over the years. Ask in your mailers for people to bring old photos and movies to the reunion and line up a few volunteers to show slides or movies three or four times during the evening (once is never enough). Have people put their names on the items that they bring (provide materials for this) and remind them to pick up their things before they leave. A projector that automatically cycles slides can be set up for a continuous showing. Don't forget to bring extra projection bulbs and an extension cord. (Tape all cords to the floor or carpet with duct tape.)

Old photos can be terribly tempting to some people. They simply MUST have that photo of themselves back in the fifth grade, and before they (and you) know it, they have slipped it into their pocket. This DOES happen, and we are talking about otherwise perfectly honest citizens. But the solution is quite simple. Place all important photos under a piece of glass. Ordinary window glass will do, although heavier glass is better. Sand sharp edges of glass with emery cloth, or cover with masking tape.

Residence Map. (See Figure 23.) This will give everyone a good overview of the class's geographical mix, and besides it's just plain fun to see where everybody lives. To create the map you will need: a map of your area within a radius of 300–400 miles, a map of the United States, long straight pins (hat pins are good), peel-off self-stick labels (½" × 1¾" is a good size), marking pen, corregated cardboard, tape, and a copy of the mailing list. Attach the maps to the cardboard with the tape. Write or type people's names on the labels, attach each label to a pin, stick the pin in the city or town of the person's current residence. Include those who are not present at the reunion. For locations where there are several people residing, make a long "pin" by straightening a paper clip, and attach the labels in a row to this clip. As you get closer to your hometown, the map will get more and more crowded until it gets ridiculous—stop at this point! You can display a typed list of everyone living too close to appear on the map, or simply display a sign explaining that those names not shown are the ones in the hometown area. Then do the same thing with the map of the U.S., excluding those who are on the more local map. Be sure to have a large table to use for this display. It can also be hung on a wall, but then the angle of the pins must be different for maximum readability. For best results, assemble the maps in the same position in which they will be displayed.

FIGURE 23. A "Residence Map" is fun as well as interesting, and also creates a place for people to "mix."

Bulletin Board/Memorabilia Table. You may want to invite people to bring photos of their families to display on a bulletin board for the evening. This makes an effective ice-breaker and will eliminate the need to be pulling wallet photos out in the middle of conversations. Each photo should be labeled for easy identification (bring labels and marking pens for this purpose). Display letters from classmates and teachers who could not attend. Solicit these letters through the mailers. You could also encourage people to bring (or send) their favorite sayings, short newspaper clippings, cartoons, etc. Again, these should be labeled with the contributor's name.

You can set up a memorabilia display on a long table or bulletin board. A table set AGAINST a bulletin board makes an even more effective display. Consider including pom-poms, school or letter sweaters (borrow a maniken from a local clothing store), old editions of the school paper, yearbooks, sports-related items such as trophies or photographs, and whatever else your imaginations and attics may yield. The best sources for these items will be your classmates (mention your search in the mailers) and the school. Arrangements for the table(s) and bulletin board(s) should be made ahead of time. If the facility has none, consider borrowing from the school or renting. They could be decorated nicely in the school colors using paper tablecloths and crepe paper.

In Memorium. There are many ways to present a memorial display. The important thing is to keep it tasteful and not have it look as if it were just thrown together. If at all possible, have photographs of the deceased. If there are just a few, give each photo or each name its own "space." Don't crowd them together. Keep it non-denominational. Flowers, of course, are always appropriate. A single votive candle is a nice touch if the local fire codes allow it. There could be a soft spotlight setting off the whole display.

The display could be somewhere near the entrance to the main room or off in a corner. The important thing is that it should be by itself with no other display or distraction nearby. It should not be a part of the general memorabilia display. School colors, mascots, or school flags should not be used.

CHAPTER IO

During the Big Day

Using Volunteers – The Registration Table – Last Minute Arrivals and No-Shows – Individual Photos – Group Photo – The Master of Ceremonies – The Program – Live Music – Awards.

Using Volunteers

The big day is approaching. You are excited and apprehensive. But try not to stretch yourself too thin—after all, you deserve to enjoy the reunion, too. Everything will go smoothly if you plan each aspect of the reunion ahead of time (just as you have been doing), **AND make sure enough volunteers are on hand to carry out the plans.**

Here is the main, number one rule for The Big Day: Get everything that is humanly possible done before the reunion. Otherwise, the committee will be too tired to enjoy the event. No one helping to set-up should work more than 2 or 3 hours the day of the reunion. And then they should have at least a 2 hour break before it begins.

A few weeks before the reunion, start rounding up volunteers by telephone. Don't ask just committee members. Also try to recruit those who were too busy to serve on the committee, but who could spend an hour or two working on the day of the reunion or at the event itself.

Some of the jobs will require prior planning and/or purchasing of materials. In this category are: decorations, refreshment table, memorabilia display, registration procedure, name tags, Master of Ceremonies, bartending, and candid photography. You should be sure that the people in charge of these areas know exactly what to do, what is expected of them, how much they can spend, etc. Talk to them by phone to find out how they are progressing. Get them the help they need (if any). Be sure they know when to set-up. Different amounts of time will be needed for different jobs. Anyone doing a job that takes more than 2 hours should be allowed to go home and rest for 2 or 3 hours before the reunion begins. For other jobs the volunteers should arrive about 1 ½ hours before the reunion. This should allow enough time for them to get last minute orientation and instructions from those in charge, survey the situation, and get set-up and mentally prepared for the rush. Some jobs require very little preparation and the volunteers can arrive just before the reunion begins. They should be instructed to check in for any last minute instructions.

WAYS TO USE VOLUNTEERS THE DAY OF THE REUNION:

- Decorating.
- Setting up tables, equipment, and displays.
- Getting change from the bank or local stores ($10's, $5's, and $1's).
- Setting up and keeping an eye on the memorabilia. Making sure everything is labeled properly and gets back to the right person.
- Bartending (if you have your own bar).
- Taking a turn at the registration table (if you don't get "outside" people to do it).
- Keeping refreshment table stocked.
- Setting up, testing, and running projectors (slide, movie).
- Setting up, testing, and running cassette tape machine.
- Setting up and testing sound system.
- Master of Ceremonies and helpers.
- Making large signs or placards for last minute announcements (for example: a raffle).
- Selling raffle tickets.
- Greeting people.
- Taking candid photographs.
- Cleaning up.

The Registration Table

The registration table will need change in the form of small bills —$10's, $5's, and $1's—for unannounced arrivals, and for those who haven't yet paid in full and forgot their check books. You may need to do this a day or two early since most banks are closed on the weekends.

Make sure the people at the registration table are well-informed about the check-in procedure, know who to hand the money to at the end of the evening, and are supplied with:

- extra blank name tags.
- marking pens.
- ballpoint pens.
- a list of who owes money.
- cash box and change.
- class surveys (for those showing up unannounced).
- someone to relieve them during the evening. (No volunteer should do this job for more than an hour—45 minutes is better. If the person is being hired, they should still be relieved occasionally.)

The first people who the new arrivals should see are the greeters, stationed at the entrance area in front of the registration table. Two or three of these people should be on hand during the first hour or two until dinner. Their only job is to make everyone feel welcome and comfortable. Toward this end, they should make light, easy conversation, over-looking no one, and reserving intense one-on-one conversation for later in the evening when they are no longer serving in the capacity of greeters. Not everyone can do this job, and even the ones who can sometimes tire of it quickly. Try to relieve these people often. No one should be a greeter for more than 30 minutes at a time.

The entrance area should be roped off or partitioned in some way so that the people arriving MUST go past the registration table to get in. All other entrances should be blocked off. If another activity is taking place simultaneously (as often happens in convention centers and large hotels), have large signs or posters pointing to your reunion. The place of registration should consist of a long table where the "business" part of the reunion takes place — such things as: money transactions; passing out name tags, photographer's cards, and surveys (to those who haven't mailed them in); and directing people to the line for individual photos.

Anyone who is not a member of the class, and is not a spouse, date, or friend of a member of the class, should wear an identifying name tag. You can photocopy and use the example on p. 115.

Last Minute Arrivals and No-Shows

Those at the registration table should be prepared to welcome people who show up at the reunion unannounced at the last minute. Why? Because some people are so nervous, they put off deciding to go until just before the event, sometimes until the night of the event. This really isn't a big problem if you plan for it. The idea is to make everyone feel comfortable even (or especially) if they are shy or nervous.

Most banquet halls require an approximate meal count up until about a half hour before dinner when they will require an exact (more or less) meal count. However, they also plan for a few extra people attending, so if people drop in unexpectedly, it should present very little problem as long as it doesn't get out of hand. And if you just don't mention this policy to your classmates, it won't get out of hand.

You can, however, mention in the mailers and through the grapevine that people can show up AFTER the dinner — tell them approximately what time it will be over. This arrangement often appeals to teachers, and to those who can't really afford to be there otherwise. Since the meal is usually the most expensive part of a reunion, the fee should be substantially less in this way, BUT it should also be made clear that everyone must pay their fair share, even the ones who claim they only want to stay for "a moment." The amount should be calculated in advance so that people at the registration table don't have to hem and haw and haggle over money.

Illness, last-minute emergencies, and last-minute jitters may cause a few no-shows. Some will expect their money back. We suggest stating a policy of NO REFUNDS in all of your mailers. Then, after the reunion, IF you have money left over you might consider refunding these people some of their money.

Individual Photos (also see p. 118)

Many reunions have individual photos taken directly after check-in. This makes the photo session part of the registration process. The advantages are:

• At this time people are fresh and look their best.

• There is less chance of someone forgetting to have a picture taken (and maybe regretting it later).

• It's easier to get people to have their picture taken BEFORE they get involved in the reunion.

The main disadvantage is:

• Having to line up right away instead of being free to roam around.

Most photographers prefer that name tags not be worn during the individual photos. Toward this end you could modify the registration procedure by handing out name tags after the photos are taken. Station a volunteer directly outside the photo-taking area to give out name tags after the people have been photographed and just before they are admitted to the main room. It also works to have the name tags spread out on a table for people to select themselves. Work out traffic flow so that people cannot get past the photographer. The registration sequence would be:

1. Register first, then receive the photographer's card.

2. Wait in line; get individual photos taken.

3. Receive name tags.

4. Enter the main room.

Although this method does take longer, once it's over people are free to talk and mingle for the rest of the evening.

Group Photo (also see p. 117)

If individual photos are taken, you should seriously consider not having a group photo taken. The combination of both can be very time consuming. The best time for a group photo is right before dinner. Not only are the maximum number of people present, but after the dinner and program comes "dance and conversation time," which is not at all conducive to photo sessions.

It takes a lot longer to organize a group photo than you might expect because people are talking, milling around, and are just generally caught up in the excitement of the event. Figure at least 30 minutes and as long as 45 minutes. You will probably need to use a public address system if your group is large. Put someone with strong leadership abilities in charge of this—not the photographer (unless he or she insists).

The Master of Ceremonies

Try to find an experienced (or at least willing) MC to coordinate the program and keep it lively. Your MC doesn't have to be a Johnny Carson or Lily Tomlin, but it helps if he or she has a good sense of humor and knows how to handle a crowd. A class officer is a likely choice, but only if she or he is enthusiastic about the reunion and willing to re-familiarize him/herself with old school activities and classmates. A volunteer MC will usually appear. If not, divide up the duties among the more outgoing members of the committee and do the best you can.

The Program

The program is the one time during the evening when everyone is focused on the same activity. If used effectively, it can create a feeling of unity; or it can become a complete bore. The difference is preparation.

For starters, keep it short—45 minutes is plenty. To pack all you will want to do in that time frame will require some organization. People at reunions are generally enthusiastic and excited, but their attention spans are short. Unless the program is fast-moving and pertinent, they will become more interested in talking to friends than in listening. And if you have ever tried to bring a room of several hundred buzzing people to order, you know how difficult it can be.

The best time for the program is usually right after the meal, while everyone is still seated. A good sound system which projects to every corner of the room is essential for any group of more than about 25. It's impossible to hold people's attention if they can't hear you—especially at a reunion. If you intend to use the microphone of the band or DJ, be sure they set up early enough. Since the music usually starts after the program, they may set up too late for your needs, unless you make prior arrangements.

A day or two before the reunion the MC should draw up a complete outline of the program and brief each participant on what he or she is expected to do and how long it should take. A short meeting, or at least several phone calls, will be necessary to accomplish this. You may want to divide up the various parts of the program and give several different people a chance to make announcements, give awards, etc. This adds interest and gives a variety of personalities a chance to express themselves. Each person in the program should carry note cards to lessen the possibility of leaving something out. The MC should introduce each participant and be back on stage leading applause as the participant is leaving so that there is no "gap" or empty stage. Before signing off, ask if anyone has a brief announcement or comment. At smaller reunions (groups of 40 or less), people sometimes stand up and talk about themselves and introduce their spouses. It also helps if the MC and all program participants remain relatively sober.

Themes, skits, speeches, and professional entertainment have no place at a bonafide reunion. An exception to this rule would be reunions that happen every year. These are more like conventions or annual meetings and different rules apply. But at a regular reunion, conversation and becoming re-acquainted is entertainment enough. If there is someone in your group who is a professional entertainer who wishes to perform, be SURE that he or she understands that the routine is to last no more than about 10 minutes.

Once the program is over, people will naturally gravitate to the dance floor, to small groups for conversation, or to the various activity centers.

HERE ARE SOME POSSIBILITIES FOR YOUR PROGRAM:

Acknowledgements. You may want to thank the organizing committee, and perhaps single out one or two people who worked especially hard. You may also want to thank any teachers or administrators present; the spouses for putting up with someone else's reunion; donors; and people who volunteered to help out during the event. A small gift may or may not be appropriate; use your discretion.

A more serious acknowledgement could be made by presenting an engraved plaque, trophy, or a quality gift. Some possibilities are:

a well-liked teacher; a classmate who has done a lot of community service; a retired principal, administrator or custodian; someone who has "pulled through" despite personal or family tragedy; a professional who has distinguished himself or herself; a past-president of your group (if you are organized into an association). These awards are best presented BEFORE any "joke" awards.

Remembering the deceased. Have a prayer or moment of silence to commemorate deceased classmates. Try to find someone in your group who is comfortable with, and articulate about, such matters — perhaps a minister, priest, rabbi, or counselor or just someone with sincere feelings and tact. At the very least, a "person of the church" within your community would surely be willing to offer advice. And do whatever you can to check out the rumors of a person's death. We have heard a LOT of stories about people showing up at their reunion to prove that "the rumors of their demise were greatly exaggerated."

Awards. Traditionally, these are almost always humorous with inexpensive or joke gifts for the lucky recipients. But it takes a light touch to pull this off well. It's best to drop any category that seems questionable. Remember, your goal is not to embarrass anyone, but for the whole class to have a good laugh on itself. See the end of this chapter for a complete list of award categories and suggestions.

If you ask the right questions, much of the information for your awards can come from the class surveys sent out in the mailers. However, be prepared to make some last-minute changes based on surveys filled out at the reunion itself. Also, you will discover that some categories will require direct observation (baldest, changed the least, last to arrive), and perhaps a few discrete questions asked during the reunion. Someone must be assigned to this task. "The Survey" in Chapter 8 will give you more information.

Speeches. The rule of thumb is to keep them short (or not have them at all). Three minutes at the most. Nothing will kill your program faster than a long-winded speech, no matter how well-intentioned or sincere the speaker.

Toasts. A toast is never necessary at a reunion, but if done right, can be quite moving and meaningful. However, it is next to impossible to explain how to give a good toast. The object or recipient of the toast, of course, would be the class as a whole. It would not be appropriate to toast an individual or smaller group within the class. The length of a good toast varies anywhere from a few words to a few minutes, though the shorter ones tend to be better. The person giving the toast should be nothing less than "completely willing" to do the job. By no means should anyone be assigned the job against his or her will, or coerced into doing it. An appropriate time for the toast would be right after the meal and before the program, or else at the end of the program just before everyone gets up to "circulate." Of course, everyone should have a glass with a bit of "spirits" in it — either wine or an after-dinner liqueur. The non-drinkers should also have a glass with spirits, though they don't have to drink. Grape juice or non-alcoholic wine would also be appropriate for such folks. The glasses need not be filled — "two fingers" worth is plenty. Most facilities will allow you to bring your own wine for "toasting purposes." This will save you a lot of money, but check first. And don't forget the corkscrew.

Inglenook Winery in Napa Valley, California, offers a red wine (bordeaux blend) entitled, "Reunion." Expensive but elegant, it may be of interest to some smaller groups. For details, see Appendix A.

Announcements. While you have a captive audience, use your time well. Remind people to make donations or buy raffle tickets if you need to raise more money — circulate the donation jar and send ticket sellers around again. Let people know who is in charge of the mailing list and remind them to send change of addresses to that person. Preview the rest of the evening. Mention the closing time. If there is an event planned for the following day — a breakfast or picnic — announce it. Let people know there is a separate area or room available for conversation (if you have live music, it usually starts right after the program.) Don't bother to ask if people want another reunion in 5 years. In the rush of the moment, everyone will say yes.

Presentation to the school. If a gift or scholarship is to be presented to the school, it is a much "classier act" if a representative of the school is present to receive the gift (traditionally in the form of a check). Someone taking flash photos of the event adds to the fanfare, even if the photos are not used (or even if there is no film in the camera, for that matter). An alternative is to stage the event (a handshake and passing the check from hand to hand) at the school or local newspaper office a few weeks before the reunion, have photos taken, and display the photos at the reunion.

Special presentations. The following verbal presentation is a wonderful example of good program entertainment. It's short and holds the attention of the audience by combining nostalgia and wit, and by comparing the past with the present. It includes "acknowledgements" in an entertaining kind of way, as well as drawings and "joke" awards. It was given by Don Gillingham and Rae Ann Dahl Bleth, co-chairs of Hudson's Bay High School, Class of '60, Vancouver, WA, at their 25th reunion. Don put together the piece getting some of his material from the World Encyclopedia 1960 annual volume, but the primary inspiration and much of the material comes directly from a speech written and given by Fred Jossy at the 25th reunion of Eagle Point High School, Eagle Point, OR, Class of '59. The dialogue, bouncing back and forth from one person to the other, gives variety and impact to the presentation. It would be relatively simple to adapt this type of thing to your own situation. (For sources of facts, figures, and trivia see "Other Embellishments" in Chapter 8, and Appendix A.)

PERSON A: Twenty-five years the other side of 1960 our country was floundering in the Great Depression. It would be six more years before Americans would become involved in World War II. Many of those people were our parents at a similar age as ourselves in 1960.

PERSON B: In 1960 you could get free road maps at service stations, gas was 20 cents a gallon, and free steak knives and glassware could be yours for purchasing 10 gallons or more.

A: Although Edsels were discontinued in 1960, you could buy a new Ford, Chevrolet or Studebaker ranging from $2,300 to $3,900.

B: In 1960 we had not become accustomed to such phrases as:

PERSON A	PERSON B
Touchtone	Time Share
800 number	Recreational drugs
Condo	Video
Zip code	Volunteer Armed Forces

A: "Hardware" was sold at Coast to Coast. (chain hardware store)

B: and "software" was sold at Hadley's. (local women's apparel store)

A: Drive Ins were the only legal place to park at night (for more than a few minutes) and "making out" is probably called something else. I don't have the nerve to ask my kids for clarification.

B: If you stayed home on Saturday night you watched Gunsmoke, Fight of the Week, Make that Spare, or Have Gun Will Travel.
   A trip to the theater (remember loge seats?) would expose you to such risque movies as: The Apartment, Elmer Gantry, Psycho, and Sparticus.
   There were no nude shots, no "R" ratings, and the movies that dared nudity were foreign, poor quality, and usually more sedate by today's standards.

A: "Grass" was what I mowed Saturdays to make extra money.
   Living together was called "shacking up" and was socially unacceptable.

B: "Gay" was just a happy person, and a "fag" was a cigarette.

A: Nobody thought of putting Coke up their nose either.
   Remember the basketball great, Oscar Robertson? Or the NBA coaches Lenny Wilkins and Jerry West? They were three of the five picked as first team College All Americans in 1960.

B: Those graduates out of college in 1960 were commanding monthly salaries of: Teaching, $375; Engineering, $600; accounting, $500. And we could hardly wait to get into that work force.

A: Prince Andrew was born in 1960, and Clark Gable died. If Clark Gable were still alive, he would be 84.
   Adolph Eichmann was captured in 1960, and stories still unfold today about the infamous persons of the Nazi regime.

B: You mailed your graduation announcements for 4 cents.

A: Yes, and made arrangements to borrow the only car that most families had.
   And the Elks made a valiant attempt to keep drinking off the streets with a graduation party.

B: I guess they could be called the original "Mothers Against Drunk Drivers," although they've been known to tip a few themselves over the years.
Elvis Presley had several of the top hits of 1960. You'll hear some of them throughout the evening.

A: You know that Rafer Johnson lit the Olympic Torch in Los Angeles last year. In 1960 he won a gold medal in Rome in the decathlon. Wilma Rudolph took 3 gold medals and Al Oerter another. Cassius Clay, who later became famous as Muhammed Ali, won a gold in boxing.

B: And now we'd like to introduce the people who worked on the reunion:

(The introductions are alternated by Person A and Person B. Each committee member's name is announced and the part of the reunion that he or she worked on is mentioned. The person stands to applause and sits down before the next person is introduced.)

A: A great deal of time and effort was put in by these people, and more to come as the reunion booklet is put together for mailing out to you in a few weeks.

B: Let's give something away! (Drawing for a mug and T-shirt.)

A: (Drawing for Life Magazine of May 30, 1960 and a T-shirt.)

B: (Presentation.) We have an official Detective Kit for this lucky person. It's appropriate because he located several missing alumni. In one case he went door to door in an old neighborhood until he found someone who remembered the parents of our classmate. In another he searched through school district retirement records. (Name withheld) come up and get your Detective Kit and T-shirt.

A: We received a nice note from one of you that said, "We'll be there, but where is the questionnaire?" The questionnaire was on the back of the note that she wrote to us. The Most Observant Alumni Award goes to (name withheld). She wins 5 pounds of junk mail and a T-shirt.

B: Here's a good one. This is for our special "Creative Writing Award." We send out a questionnaire and she sends back a book. Here are some excerpts: "Hobbies: Tennis, running, avoiding housework." Or from "Highlights of the last 10 years": "Joining an outlaw biker club with my Honda Passport." Or: "Experiments always in progress in Tupperware containers in back of refrigerator," and "Trying to save enough money to come to this lousy reunion." We give this writing tablet and box of pencils to (name withheld).

A and B: May health and happiness follow you through the next 25 years.

Live Music

Dance music usually starts after the program is over. As we have mentioned many times, you will want to have a separate area or room where people can talk, far enough away from the band to allow comfortable conversation. If you still find the music too loud, ask the band to play more quietly. You might discuss this possibility with the band leader beforehand. That way if you must do it, it won't seem so awkward. If you are using a DJ instead of a band, this will be much easier (it's just a volume control). It's very important that people are able to talk without shouting.

Award Categories and Ideas

The number of winners can be increased by having "men" and "women" awards for each category; also, "runners-up" awards. We are listing more than you can possibly use, so pick the ones most appropriate for your group. For more information on awards see: "The Program," this chapter; and "The Survey," in Chapter 8.

AWARD CATEGORIES:

Most recently married (Newlywed Award)
Longest married (to same person)
Most married
Classmates married to each other
Most eligible single person

Most recent parent
Parent with most children
Award for twins or triplets
Parent with largest number of boys in family

Parent with largest number of girls in family
Parent with oldest child
Newest in-law
Newest grandparent
First to become a grandparent
Person with most grandchildren
Newest great-grandparent
First great-grandparent
Most great-grandchildren

Most unusual occupation
First to retire
Highest military rank
Most number of years in military

Traveled longest distance to reunion
Traveled shortest distance
Person who changed home address the most
First to make reservation (Promptness Award)
Last arrival (Procrastinator Award)

Most improved
Person who weighs closest to high school weight
Man with smoothest head (Chrome Dome Award)
Person who has changed the least (The Time Stood Still Award or
    The Golden Clone Award)

General door prize(s)

Many of the above categories are humorous in nature as are the
awards or gifts. Examples of humorous "gifts" are: ear plugs for the
most recent parent; an apron for the most recently married man;
toy watch for the first to retire; comb with no teeth for baldest man;
coffee cup marked "Grandpa" for first grandfather; etc.

A witty person can think of many more, but the important thing
is that they be inexpensive (and don't forget to budget for them).
Other possibilities include: plaques, trophies, and loving cups made
of plastic or wood and available from novelty shops, mail order
houses, and 5 and 10's. Also, check handicraft stores, and trophy
shops. Artistic volunteers can create paper certificates, needlepoint
wall hangings, or paper mache gifts and trophies.

Non-joke awards could be on display during the reunion.

Should you award a door prize using the under-the-seat method, have the MC announce at the appropriate time that there is a label under a certain chair and point out this chair. This is much better than the disruptive activity of having everyone stand up and turn over their chairs. Of course, this whole scheme works only if people are free to choose their own seats.

Possibilities for general door prizes: gifts from local businesses (important to mention their name during presentation), floral table centerpieces, free admission to the next reunion.

CHAPTER 11

After It's Over

The Next Day – Loose Ends.

The Next Day

Occasionally a group that has a dinner/dance reunion will hold an event the next day—usually a picnic or BBQ that allows for a more casual atmosphere and perhaps includes the children. It all sounds like a wonderful idea, and it is. But despite the best intentions, attendance at these events is normally lower than expected, especially if alcohol was available the night before. That shouldn't discourage your plans; just don't be upset if fewer people attend than said they would. It helps to have it as late in the day as possible. Start at noon for a lunch event, and around 4 p.m. for a dinner event (that should still leave enough daylight—at least in the summer).

For some people, the 6 or 8 hours that a reunion lasts are simply not enough. It's not uncommon for people to gather at someone's house or at an all-night restaurant after the reunion is over and stay up talking until morning. Regardless of their original intentions, these people will probably not be showing up for a planned event the next day. Also, by the next day the excitement about getting together has worn off and people are ready to be on their way. Ten years later you can get together and do it all again!

Loose Ends

Watch out for PRS! Post Reunion Syndrome. The person affected worst is usually the one in charge of the memory book. A directory must be put together; a montage page made up of photos taken at the reunion; a memorial page; and a letter from the committee. And the later this is done, the later the memory book will be completed and sent out.

The final bookkeeping must be done. Pay and collect the final debts. After all checks have cleared, close the checking account and, if money is left over, put it into a savings account with two or more signatures required for withdrawal.

Put the files in order and then in a safe place—along with a copy of the memory book, video, scrapbook, and group gift or memento. A separate address list with phone numbers should kept in a different safe place (the directory in the memory book may serve this purpose, if it's complete).

One last task for the committee: You might want to telephone or send brief hand-written notes thanking those who volunteered their time or donated items for the reunion. And, since you, the reunion organizers, played the most important roles in making the reunion a success, consider having a post-reunion evaluation session and celebration (a party!!!) over lunch or dinner. Use your own discretion, but most reunion committees do not consider it unethical to use left-over funds to finance these celebrations. You deserve it!

And now that you are experts, you can help us make the next edition of this book more comprehensive and useful for other organizers by sending us helpful hints, anecdotes, examples, suggestions and criticisms. Tell us what worked and what didn't work for you. If your input is useful, it will appear in the next edition of this book.

PART II

Special Types of Reunions

In this part of the book you will find help with four types of reunions that are distinctively different from the typical public school reunion. They are:

CHAPTER 12

Military Reunions

*Introduction – The Preliminary Stage – The Reunion Is "On" –
Location of the Reunion – Length of the Reunion – Choosing a
Facility – Mailers/Newsletters – Travel/Transportation – Finding
People – Grapevine Leads – The Forwarded Letter – Using the
Media – Military Orders – Electronic Bulletin Boards –
Commercial Electronic Networks – Military Locators – The
Reunion Schedule – Forming a Non-Profit Organization –
Imprinted Memorabilia and Giftware.*

This chapter is dedicated to:

**The 29 million American Veterans,
and to Col Tom Crawford (USAF Ret) and
LtCol Sid Johnston (USAF Ret) of
The Mosquito Assn, Inc. (6147th Tactical Control Group).**

This chapter is for those of you who are planning a military
reunion. At the beginning of this book you were instructed to read
this part first, which you should do. BUT the information and tips
you find here are SUPPLEMENTAL to the rest of the book. Much of
the information about school reunions can be directly applied to
military reunions. What you will find in this section is information
more or less exclusive to, or of particular interest to, military
reunion organizers.

This chapter (in fact, this whole book) was written with the
beginner in mind. The idea is to give the novice an overall perspective of the possibilities and techniques, which should still allow an
experienced person to select some useful points and ideas.

Introduction

Those of you who served in the military know that those years were among the most intense, unforgettable, and influential of your life. And the largest part of that experience, the part that keeps coming back time and again, is the people — those men or women you served with. Served with? What a strange term. That actually meant eating, working, playing, joking, yelling, suffering and celebrating together, day in and day out. Good times, bad times, great times, boring times, and times that literally scared you to death. At first you were strangers but you became friends, even with some you might have avoided or never met in "the real world."

But it was more than friendship. Your present sense of camaraderie and nostalgia is not really focused around happy and casual memories like those of high school, such as rooting for the home team or getting together at the local hamburger joint, but on uncommon bonds forged under unusual conditions. You depended on each other to get the job done; you needed each other to survive battles and boredom, and you came away with an experience known only to those who have been there.

Then, many of you were catapulted from military service directly back into civilian life. After your discharge or retirement, you scattered to towns and cities across America. When you try to remember your military experience and the people you served with, there are blank spots and a sense of incompleteness because no one is around to remember with you, and there is a lot you have forgotten. Your experiences and thoughts may not be easily shared with people you now love and live with. Friends and family may have long ago begun to yawn over old war stories, never realizing their subtle yet profound importance to you. A reunion offers you a chance to remember, fill in the blanks, rediscover long-lost friends, compare experiences, ask a friend that important question, spend time with someone you had previously overlooked, be with those who understand, and finally put into proper perspective that most profound and powerful part of your life.

*   *   *   *   *

We would like your help. When it comes to military reunions, there are sure a lot of old pros out there — people who have organized reunions for years and who could write this chapter three times over. If you are such a person, we would like to hear from you. Send us your suggestions, additions, criticisms, and experiences. Put us on your mailing list so that we can receive your newsletters, press kits, new-member packets, etc. We update this book about every three years, and we would certainly like to add your input to the next edition. In fact, with your help, this chapter may very well become a book of its own.

The Preliminary Stage

With most first-time reunions there is a preliminary stage — that time between when you "think" there is going to be a reunion and when you "know" there is going to be one. With military reunions this preliminary stage can last a long time, even several years, and its main focus is on finding people. Only when you have found enough people who are interested in attending a reunion can you actually start planning your reunion. Once a deposit (usually non-refundable) has been made for a facility, the preliminary stage comes to an end and the "real" reunion planning begins.

Many military reunions are organized by retired military people or business people with experience in management. Such people have good organizing skills, are familiar with using the media, know about long-distance communications, have contacts around the country, and have the time and desire to search for people. But if you don't have such skills, don't despair. Only one skill is really needed to spearhead a reunion: the ability to find and orchestrate people who DO have the necessary skills. Just don't pretend to be an expert and everything should be okay.

Generally, you will begin by locating and then telephoning a few of your service buddies to find out what they think of the idea of a reunion, and to ask them to help find others. Buy them their own copy of this book. Also get a copy of one of the best books on the subject, *You Can Find Anyone,* also available from us (see p. 221).

With military reunions, it can be difficult for a committee to meet, given the fact that the members are likely to be scattered all over the country. In the preliminary stages, your meetings may have to take place through phone calls and letters unless some of you live within driving distance of each other. (A conference call system, called "3-way calling," is available on most residential private lines with touch-tone dialing.) Once you get to the reunion stage, schedule a meeting of the committee the day before, or the morning before, the reunion begins. Formal associations and organizations schedule board and committee meetings before, during, or after the reunion, depending upon their preferences and by-laws.

You should consider starting a newsletter at this point. As your group grows larger, a newsletter becomes the cheapest and most effective way of tying people together and keeping the interest up. However, it DOES require someone with time and ability. Chapter 8 gives tips and resources on how to design and paste-up a newsletter. Read it carefully and then send for some of the resources, catalogs, and books mentioned in Appendix A.

Some people are put off by the whole idea of creating a newsletter. They think that it's more work and bother than it's worth, or in some cases they are just not cut out for that kind of work and they drive themselves nuts trying to do it. But you have to mail something out anyway. A common, average mailer could be spruced up a bit and made to resemble a small newsletter. It doesn't have to be pages and pages long. An 8 ½ × 11 sheet of paper with a nice letterhead, maybe a columnized format and reduced type (see Figures 10A and 10B), printed on both sides or maybe even one side, is good enough for starters. As interest accumulates and your group gets larger, perhaps someone will volunteer who can do more. One other tip: The "voice" or perspective of a newsletter should be from "you" as a group rather than "you" as an individual.

This is the time to start sending "looking for" announcements to publications pertaining to your branch of the service. See the back of this chapter for an example, and Appendix B for a list of these publications.

The Reunion Is "On"

After a period of time of concerted effort, ranging anywhere from a few weeks to a few years, depending on your particular situation, the day arrives when you finally decide to go ahead with the reunion. You have gathered enough information and have found enough people so that you feel reasonably assured of success. At this point, tentatively schedule the reunion for at least a year in advance; 18–24 months is even better. Here are some things to consider at this time:

Location of the Reunion. Most military groups do not have a particular place to return to as with high school reunions. However, there are exceptions to this rule. If you have a ship, barracks, headquarters, air base, etc., to return to, and especially if this is your first reunion, then of course you should try to have your reunion at or near such a place, provided it isn't half way around the world.

However, if yours is like most military reunions and you haven't such a place to return to, then your basis for choosing a location should be primarily "convenience," for both the organizers and those attending. If this is your first reunion, then you can be excused for leaning a bit towards "convenience for the organizers," as long as it doesn't inconvenience too many in your group. Perhaps you could have it somewhere near the residence of the person in charge of the reunion, for example. Then as you get some experience under your belt, with future reunions you could move farther afield. If at all possible, always try to have it near a major metropolitan airport.

If you continue having reunions, then sooner or later you may have to choose a facility sight-unseen in a city you have never been to. For this reason many military reunions take place in convention centers, or in large hotels that have convention facilities, near large metropolitan airports. A simple phone call can put you in touch with the facility manager who will gladly take care of many of the details, such as: accomodations, food, refreshments, photographer, music, sound system, projectors and screens, and in some cases, decorations. You would be left with: locating people, mailing notices, collecting money, and planning the program. (Call or write the local Chamber of Commerce for a list of convention facilities. Also see about *The National Directory of Addresses and Telephone Numbers,* and *The Directory of 800 Numbers* in Appendix A.)

The "trade-off" for such convenience is, of course, money. The less you do yourself, the more your reunion will cost. But most military reunions are of this type for two good reasons: 1. The reunion usually takes place in a city far distant from the main organizer(s). If you live in Seattle and the reunion is to take place in St. Louis, then you really have no choice but to use the above method of contacting a convention center. 2. Those who attend military reunions are usually older people or retirees. These people want the conveniences of convention centers and are, in most cases, willing and able to pay for it.

If you have reunions on a continuing basis, they can take place in different cities around the country. A new location presents both novelty and the opportunity for the reunion to eventually get near enough to everyone involved. A common pattern is to have the first reunion on (let's say) the West Coast, the next one somewhere in the middle of the country, followed by the East Coast, then back to the middle, then the West Coast again, etc. Also, within each of these three sections, you could vary the locations between the north and the south.

Another possibility is to divide the country into sections as shown in Figure 24, and to rotate among these sections, picking a different city within each section, taking into account where most members are located. This is the method used by The Mosquito Association, Inc. (Korean War). They insist on having a volunteer "reunion commander" from the chosen city. If no one volunteers, a different city is chosen. Members of the association's board meet in person with the reunion commander to select the hotel/motel and then continue to communicate by mail and phone until the week of the reunion. The board members then arrive early for the reunion, have their board meeting before the reunion starts, and thus have a typed agenda ready for the reunion business meeting.

Another thing to consider is locations or sites that would be of special interest to your group. For example: The Air Force Museum at Wright-Patterson Air Force Base near Dayton, Ohio has more than 200 aircraft and missiles on display dating from the early nineteen hundreds to the present. This obviously would be a great place for a reunion of the Army Air Corps or the Air Force. Other suggestions are:

• The Red Barn Museum, Boeing Field, Seattle, WA.

• USAF Academy, Colorado Springs, CO.

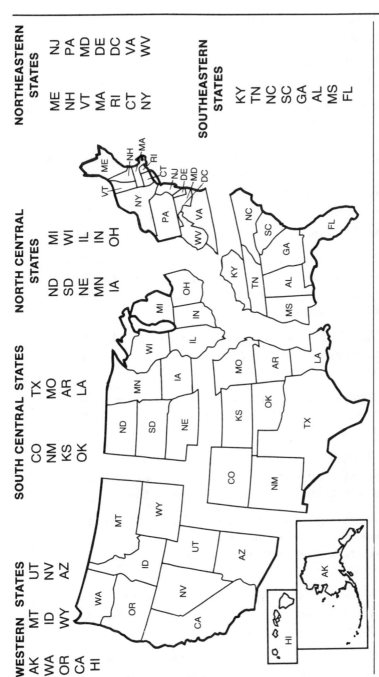

WESTERN STATES
AK   UT
WA   NV
OR   AZ
CA
HI
ID
WY

SOUTH CENTRAL STATES
CO   TX
NM   MO
KS   AR
OK   LA

NORTH CENTRAL STATES
ND   MI
SD   WI
NE   IL
MN   IN
IA   OH

NORTHEASTERN STATES
ME   NJ
NH   PA
VT   MD
MA   DE
RI   DC
CT   VA
NY   WV

SOUTHEASTERN STATES
KY
TN
NC
SC
GA
AL
MS
FL

FIGURE 24. Section map of U.S.—for choosing reunion locations, and/or showing membership distribution. For the latter, write in the proper number next to each state. Please photocopy for your own use. (After an example provided by the Mosquito Assn.)

- US Military Academy, West Point, NY.

- Air Museum, San Diego, CA.

- Patriots Point Naval Maritime Museum, Patriots Point, SC (near Charleston).

Length of the Reunion. Most military reunions last longer than the typical school reunion. One day is simply not enough time to satisfy the emotional needs of the participants. And because the majority of the people must travel, it's not enough time to justify the time and expense of the trip. Most events are at least two days long, the average is three. Four days is a bit on the long side. You don't want it too short, but too long is worse.

When Choosing a Facility. Here are some things to consider:

1. Facilities in outlying areas are usually much cheaper than those in downtown metropolitan areas. Get a map of the area you have in mind and write or call the Chambers of Commerce in some of the smaller outlying towns.

2. Ask the facility manager for the names and phone numbers of other reunion organizers who have recently used the facility. Call these people for their opinions.

3. If you have a representative of your group living in the area, have him check out each facility in person. Give him a list of what to look for.

4. Read the "List of Questions to Ask When Talking with the Manager of a Facility" in the back of Chapter 2. This list is for school reunions, but could easily be modified for your own needs.

5. Ask for a group rate and a block of rooms. Talk with at least five different facilities within your chosen area. When you get the lowest rate, call the others back to see if they can "do better." Often they can.

6. Always ask what "freebies" are available. Every facility has its own rules in this regard. The most common "freebie" is a free room for every so many paid rooms.

7. Be careful of extra costs. A general meeting room, board meeting room, hospitality room, donuts and coffee, slide projector, extra

tables and chairs, etc., can all vary in cost from free to much more than they are worth. Also be careful of "overtime" costs. Discuss every detail with the manager. With a little persuasion, some of the above items might be tossed in as "freebies."

8. ALWAYS have the facility prepare a contract. Then you can be assured that you both agree on details, prices, guaranteed attendances, "freebies," etc.

9. Ask them to send you: a floor plan of the main room, a map of the area which shows the airport(s) and train stations, written driving directions on how to find the facility, an entree and food list with prices, and a list of other services and conveniences offered by the facility.

Mailers/Newsletters. These are covered quite thoroughly in Chapter 8, and earlier in this chapter we explained why we think they are important. The difference with military reunions is that you are likely to send a lot more than two (as recommended for school reunions). During the long preliminary stage of most military reunions, you should send a mailer out at least every six months to keep the interest up. Just explain the progress being made, how many new people have been found, particular problems that have come up, ask for help, etc. Then when your reunion is actually in the works, you can use the following tips:

Most hotels have registration cards that they will send you (in bulk) to be included in your mailers. These cards are for room reservations only and are mailed directly to the hotel. You must include a separate reunion registration form in your mailer to be returned to YOU along with the registration fee. A day or two before the reunion you should check with the hotel to see if anyone registered for a room but didn't bother to register for the reunion. It happens!

The last mailer before the reunion should contain:

- a hand-drawn or simplified map showing the hotel/facility, airport(s), train station(s), and main highways.
- written driving directions on how to find the hotel/facility.
- phone numbers of car rental companies; hotel courtesy van schedule and phone number.

- approximate cost of a taxi.
- bus or limo prices and phone numbers.
- what kind of weather to expect.

This information can be obtained from the hotel/facility. Also include a schedule of reunion activities, and a reminder to bring old photos, uniforms and other memorabilia.

Travel/Transportation. Of course, the easiest thing is to allow people to arrange their own travel and transportation. But you might also consider going through a travel agent or directly through an airline company. Group rates are available, and if you have enough volume you may qualify for a "freebie." Most common of these is a "site inspection ticket," which is a free round trip ticket to your chosen city for the purpose of checking it out ahead of time. Other possible "perks" are a free rental car or a gratis ticket for every so many tickets sold. Almost all airlines offer discount car rentals to individuals who are part of a group that has signed up for group discounts. The savings per ticket varies between 5% and 40%, depending on the number in your group, the city that you choose for your reunion, the time of year, and whether you have used that airline in the past. If you stay with one airline for two or three reunions, you will eventually qualify for their highest discount. The minimum number of people who can qualify for group discounts varies widely, but some airlines will go as low as ten.

Many travel agents and most airline companies have 800 numbers. The following toll free numbers can be used to sign up for group discounts:

American Airlines: 800/227-2537, 8–5, M–F, Central Time.
Eastern or Continental Airlines: 800/468-7022, 8–9, M–F, Eastern Time.
Delta Airlines: 800/241-6108, 8–5, M–F, Eastern Time.
Northwest Airlines: 800/328-2216, 7:30–5, M–F, Central Time.
Piedmont Airlines: 800/334-8644, 8:30–6, M–F, Eastern Time.
   (From NC or Canada call: 800/251-5720.)
Trans World Airlines: 800/TWA-MEET, 7:30–7, M–F, Central Time.
United Airlines: 800/633-8825, 8:30–6, M–F, Eastern Time.

Finding People (also see Chapter 6)

It is important both before and after the preliminary stage, to put time, money and effort into finding people. If you decide to have reunions on a continuing basis, then this process should be considered unending. One person should be in charge of finding people and his name, address, and phone number should be in all your mailings and correspondence. He should have year-round authority and funding to do research by mail and telephone. And, of course, he should be willing and able to do such research. Such a person (or persons, if you are lucky enough to have more than one in your group) is perhaps your greatest asset, especially in the formative years of your organization. If he has a computer to help with maintaining the files, so much the better. However, there are other techniques that can be used (see Chapter 7).

These "locator" people are mainly interested in four things:

1. A list of all the people in their group.

2. The full name and other identifying information of each person.

3. Is the person still alive?

4. If so, the whereabouts of the person.

The means available for obtaining the above information can be described as follows:

1. The grapevine. Gathering information by talking or corresponding with people and tapping their memory.

2. The media. Using newspapers, newsletters, magazines, radio and TV to make announcements and ask questions.

3. Historic sources, both private and government. These sources are good for adding to the list of people who were part of your group, and determining if a person was killed in action or survived. The addresses obtained from these sources are usually too old to be of any use. In this category are: unit histories, necrologies (lists of deceased), military orders, old letters and photos, newspaper articles listing those deceased and those returning, rosters, POW records, diaries, and inactive (no longer updated) military files. In this latter category are the Military Personnel files in The National

Personnel Records Center in St. Louis, MO, which supposedly contain records on every person who was ever in the military (at least in modern times). The bad news is that the average person (especially civilian) has no access to these records. The good news is that the addresses, especially of those who did their hitch and got out, are very old and most likely useless. Figure 25 shows the type of response you are likely to get back from them.

4. Current (updated) military files. All branches of the service keep records on their active duty, retired, and Reserve personnel. These files are maintained by the various "Military Locators" (see p. 173 and Appendix B).

5. Private and non-military sources. These are covered at the end of Chapter 6.

Grapevine Leads. You will face the challenge of locating veterans who may be scattered evenly across the country or the world — unlike school reunions where 50% of the people live within 50 miles of the hometown. And though some friends may have kept in

REPLY TO INQUIRY (NCP)

DATE

SUBJECT:
Returned Request/Unable To Forward

Your reference

Date of inquiry

The answer to your inquiry is furnished below. This abbreviated form of reply has been adopted as a means of supplying information speedily.

We regret that we are unable to provide a forwarding service on requests of this nature. Many hours are required to search for the records, extract the latest address in each, and then address and mail the envelopes. It is important to note that the addresses in military records are usually those furnished by the veteran at the time of discharge and do not usually remain valid for more than a few months. As a result, a significant amount of mail forwarded by using the last available address would be returned as undeliverable.

We are, therefore, returning your request without action.

We understand that some individuals have had success in locating former members of the military by placing advertisements in publications of various veterans' organizations such as the American Legion and Veterans of Foreign Wars.

NCPM

NATIONAL PERSONNEL RECORDS CENTER
☐ Military Personnel Records
9700 Page Boulevard
St. Louis, MO 63132
☐ Civilian Personnel Records
111 Winnebago Street
St. Louis, MO 63118

NATIONAL ARCHIVES AND RECORDS ADMINISTRATION NA FORM 13018-H (4-88)

FIGURE 25. Most requests sent to the National Personnel Records Center in St. Louis, MO, get this type of response.

touch with each other, you will find that most have not. Still, you will discover that the grapevine will most likely be your greatest source, especially if you learn to ask the right questions.

There is a very good chance that former friends actually have the information necessary to find a person — they just don't know it. And in some cases it is the combined information from two or three former friends that may eventually lead to a "find." It's your job to orchestrate this process and pull the information out of people. The "seeker" must be willing to constantly pry people with questions that will lead to useable answers: "Did he ever mention what school he went to?" "Do you recall his middle name?" "You say his dad was a farmer. Did he ever mention wanting to someday take over the farm?" (this means he may still be in his hometown area). The usefulness of pulling information from people in this way cannot be over-emphasized. If done right, this technique can lead to 80–90% of the people you are looking for.

The most important point to remember and get across to others is that **any small clue can help.** On a person's record, list all the people who knew him well. When you talk to a new contact, ask for a list of the people he knew the best. Keep this list of questions by the phone, and be sure to ask them when you make or receive a call:

LIST OF QUESTIONS TO ASK REGARDING A MISSING PERSON:

1. Names of his best friends.
2. His hometown or hometown area.
3. His job specialty.
4. Schools he attended.
5. Special interests or training.
6. Approximate age.
7. Father's occupation.
8. Nickname and middle name.
9. Religious affiliation.

ALSO, ASK THE PERSON YOU ARE TALKING TO:

1. Do you have any old photos? (Look for service numbers on the uniforms or names written on the back of the photo.)
2. Did you keep any military orders? (See p. 171.)
3. Do you have any old letters that might mention names or help you to remember.

Once you have a "hometown," a letter or phone call to the hometown Chamber of Commerce or library will get you the names of the local high schools (also get the names of local newspapers while you are at it). Writing or calling the school secretary may get you a free check into the school records (of course, it helps to know the approximate year of graduation, or age if the person didn't graduate). The address you will receive is the parents' or guardians' address at the time the person was in school, which could be very old and useless. However, the school record can also yield some very useful information, such as: full name, birthdate, full names of parents and their occupations.

Also ask the school secretary for the addresses and phone numbers of the contact people representing any reunions to be held for graduating classes plus-or-minus 6–8 years from the year you are looking for. Class reunions are great sources of information and the organizers have done the work for you. The plus-or-minus 6–8 years allows for finding siblings or cousins with the same last name. Of course, this works best with unusual or uncommon last names.

With a person's full name and birthdate you could conduct a driver's license search in the home state and neighboring states. However, these searches cost anywhere from $1 to $6 each depending on the state, payable regardless of whether the search is successful. A few states don't allow such searches, and some require the full name plus driver's license number, which you probably won't have. Also see p. 62.

Let's say you have the parents' first names and the father's occupation. You could place an ad in the local paper that reads like this: "Army buddies looking for James Q. Doe, age 48, graduate of Hometown High School, class of '56, son of John and Mary Doe, father employed as carpenter. Please write: (give address) or call collect (give phone number)." The father's occupation helps in this case because all the retired carpenters and the retired carpenter's wives are going to be racking their brains trying to remember John Doe who had a son named James. Also in such a case you might try the local carpenter's union. The name and address of the local newspaper(s) can be found through the hometown Chamber of Commerce or library. You can also find the name and address of any newspaper or magazine in the U.S. through *Ayers Book of Publica-*

tions, or *The IMS Directory of Publications* in your local library. These directories are indexed by location (as well as other ways), so you don't need to know the name of a newspaper in order to find the address.

The above methods will work only if you know the hometown or hometown area of the person in question. But it should be understood that many people far from home will say that their hometown is a large, well-known city, when in fact it's some smaller town maybe as far away as 100–150 miles from the well-known city. There is no deception intended here—it's simply a matter of convenience. It saves having to explain to someone not familiar with their area exactly where the small town is located. Then when they meet someone from their area, they invariably explain exactly where they are from. For this reason it's important to interrogate people who are supposedly from the same large city as someone you are trying to find. Even if such people never became friends, if they met even once, chances are good that they talked about the exact places that they came from. And the chances are also good that these facts will be remembered even years later. After all, finding someone from your home area is not an everyday occurance.

So for these reasons, the smaller the hometown, the better your chances of finding a person through the above methods. If you are faced with finding a person from Los Angeles (for example) and have no other clues, your best chances may be through the state or federal level rather than through the local level (with the possible exception of voting records at the county courthouse).

Other Tips. From at least the late 1940's until the Privacy Act of 1974, the Army (and very likely the other branches of the military) printed an annual list of all its officers: active, retired, and Reserve. This list included date of birth, rank, service number, full name, and address. These lists still exist in base and post libraries throughout the U.S., some dated as late as 1976.

According to the Pentagon, most military retirees live in Texas, California, Florida, Maryland, and Virginia (especially around Washington, DC). And many of them live within 30 miles of a military base in order to make use of its facilities. Checking the phone books of such areas could be worthwhile if the person is retired from the military.

The Forwarded Letter. Most colleges, trade schools, large corporations, unions, fraternal organizations, The Veterans Administration (see below), etc., are willing to forward a stamped envelope if the person in question is in their files. The "forwarded letter" approach is one of the best investments available to you. The cost is two stamps, two envelopes, and some paper. Be sure to include all pertinent information in your "front" letter, and it really helps to throw in some phrases like: "last resort," "I've been looking for this person for 5 years," "you're my only hope," "I know you are extremely busy, but ... ," etc. See "Military Locators" (below) for a detailed description of the procedure.

The Veterans Administration will search its nation-wide files, and forward a letter, if you send just one or two requests. Don't mention that it's for a reunion, and don't use letterhead stationery. The service is provided primarily for relatives to get in touch with each other and should not be abused. Send as much information as possible to your regional office (there are 58 such offices nation-wide) c/o The Privacy Act Officer. A person must be currently registered for benefits from the VA to be in their files. Someone with a service-related disability is likely to be registered.

Using the Media. Military reunions clearly do not have the "home-town advantage" that school reunions have when it comes to announcements in local newspapers and on the radio. Sending your press releases to small town newspapers and radio stations is a waste of time and money unless there is some type of "local angle," such as: your ship was home-ported nearby, your group was stationed at a nearby military base, a commander (or other well-known person in your group) was a hometown boy, your ship or aircraft was named for a nearby town or a local hero, etc. If there IS such a local angle, then the chances are very good that the newspaper or radio station will want more than just a bare-bones minimum announcement. Send them a few paragraphs on the military history of your group, the history of your reunion group, names of commanders and decorated personnel, as well as the dates of your reunion (if known), the fact that you are looking for more people, and the name, address and phone number of a contact person.

Most large metropolitan daily newspapers will not print reunion announcements, though there are exceptions to this rule. In some cases they gather them together and print them all at once. The smaller papers and the weeklies are always more obliging.

We are compiling a list of all newspapers, magazines, newsletters, radio and TV stations, and electronic bulletin boards that will print or broadcast reunion announcements. Please send us your input and information.

There are many military, government, veteran, and retiree publications that will accept **reunion announcements at no charge.** You should send announcements to these publications in both the preliminary and later stages of your reunion planning. In the preliminary stage it would be a "looking-for" announcement. After a date has been set for your reunion, you would send a reunion announcement (see the back of this chapter for examples). Be sure to contact only those publications that pertain to your branch of the service—don't (for example) bother an Army magazine for a Navy reunion. Keep your announcements brief and to the point, send them in plenty of time before your reunion, and pay attention to the deadline for each magazine or newsletter. These deadlines vary from a few days to several months before publication. See the listing in Appendix B. A big advantage of these publications is that many of the readers have a rather helpful and "fraternal" attitude in that they will go out of their way to pass on information to others who may eventually be of help. The Army Times, Air Force Times, and Navy Times (includes Marines) are the most well-read and will give you the best overall response.

Here is a tip that works well with small-town newspapers or small community newspapers (it's useless for large papers): Have **special press releases** available for attendees to pick up at the reunion. These releases, which have a blank space for people to fill in their names and hometown, explain about the reunion, give a bit of history of the group, etc. They are sent back to the hometown newspaper right after the reunion is over, and if they are printed, are often directly responsible for finding new members from the paper's readership. If at all possible, send a black-and-white photo of the attendees along with the press release. See Figure 26.

PRESS RELEASE: MOSQUITO REUNION: T-6 "TEXAN" Combat Crews,
Korean War, 6147 Tactical Control Group, 5th Air Force.

(Mr. and Mrs., Mr., Ms.) _____ ,
(a) resident(s) of (city/state) _____ ,
and a native of (city/state) _____ ,
have (has) just returned from a USAF reunion of the world famous USAF-UN "Mosquitos" in Seattle,
WA. Approximately 300 former members of the Korean War were in attendance.

"Mosquitos" refers to the unique call sign later adopted as the name of all the T-6 outfits in
Korea that flew spotter missions for the fighter-bombers of all United Nations during the Korean
War. With their Army observers these pilots flew as pathfinders behind the enemy lines, locating
enemy tanks, trucks, supply bunkers, troops, ships and train railcars. The Mosquitos marked these
targets with smoke rockets, so the speedy jet bombers could see the targets and destroy them with
minimum time over hostile territory. It was hazardous duty, but essential to the success of the
troops on the ground. The South Korean Army veterans of the Korean War still say that the brave
deeds of the "Mosquito" warrior aviators contributed much to the freedom of their country.

The Mosquito Organization is attempting to locate former "Mosquitos" who still are missing from
the reunion roll call. The Unit Alumni President of the USAF 6147 Tactical Control Group is urging
anyone who was a member or assigned on temporary duty during the Korean War to get in touch with:
Mosquito Locator Control, 6909 Rosewood Rd. NE, Albuquerque, NM 87111, 505/821-7048.

- END -

FIGURE 26. *This type of press release can be provided at the reunion for members to send back to their hometown newspaper(s). The smaller papers are more likely to print this sort of thing. Accompanying black-and-white photos will increase the chances of publication. Good for finding new members. (Example provided by the Mosquito Assn., Inc.)*

Also, there are a WHOLE LOT of military reunion organizations already out there. It may just be that your group has already formed a reunion organization—they just can't find you. If your group was in the Army, send for the free publication, "Roster of Organizations," available from: HQDA (SAPA-CR), Washington, D.C., 20310. This publication lists hundreds of veterans organizations and associations that are or were affiliated with the U.S. Army. However, it is rarely updated and as a result contains many old and useless addresses along with the good ones. Once your group is established, send them your address for inclusion in the next edition.

Also check the Armed Forces Reunion BBS, and the Service Reunions National Registry. Details are in Appendix B.

Military Orders. Everyone who was ever in the military has received Military Orders. In fact, the very first Orders for many people are to report to basic training. Then, throughout a person's "hitch" or career, there are other Orders, such as: change of assignment, change of job or duty specialty code, temporary additional duty, special training or classes, and many others. A copy of any and all orders are kept in an individual's personnel file, and that file follows the person from assignment to assignment. If a person is in the military for many years, the file may become quite large, in which case the local personnel office may choose to return some of the paperwork to the individual. And upon discharge or retirement, the person receives a copy of the file. Therefore, if the person has not thrown away these papers, they are probably still in his possession, tucked away in some remote corner. You should ask all the people in your group to send you copies of their old Orders because often they contain the names, ranks, and serial numbers of others who received the same Orders. These "others" are probably a part of your group and can be checked off against your list of "found" members. The new ones go into the "Where R U" file. Some orders contain a home address for each individual listed. These addresses are old, of course, but worth a try.

Electronic Bulletin Boards. Electronic Bulletin Board Services (BBS's) have come into existance in the last few years as a result of developing technology in personal computers and telecommunications. They are owned and operated by particular "interest groups," and are usually run out of people's homes on personal computers, and at no financial gain. With these services anyone with a personal computer, a telephone, and a modem can leave ("post") messages or receive messages, just like on a bulletin board. You can leave a reunion announcement, search for a reunion announcement, announce that you are looking for a specific person or persons, gather helpful information, or ask any question from the comfort of your own computer desk. Then you can check in from time to time to see if anyone has left a message for you in response to your previous messages. The cost is free except for any long distance phone calls.

Once you have "tapped in" to the BBS through your telephone line via the modem, instructions appear on your screen explaining how to "log on," give a password, and browse through the various sections, files, and messages that are stored in the BBS. Anyone can leave a message for anyone else or for the general public. Finding your way around the board will be slow and confusing at first, but it doesn't take too long to become reasonably proficient.

Many BBS's have listings of other BBS's that may of interest to the caller, and the people in charge of many of these BBS's are in contact with each other on a regular basis, exchanging information. This means that contacting just one or two can net you not only a lot of other contact information (other BBS's, reunion groups, publications, etc.), but can spread your message(s).

But not every "military BBS" that you find will necessarily be appropriate for posting reunion notices. Every BBS exists for specific reasons and purposes that are usually explained on the screen during the first few minutes after "logging on." Some of them are there simply to allow veterans to contact each other; others have a particular orientation or ax to grind; others try to be helpful in any way they can. And although you can post pretty much any message on any of them, very few have a section specifically for reunions. In fact, so far we have found only one: The Armed Forces Reunion BBS run by the USS Merrill Reunion Assn. (See Appendix B for details.)

A book entitled *Veterans Survival Manual* will be published sometime in mid-1989. In it is a chapter called "The Electronic Veteran," which will explain in detail the options available to the vet with a computer and modem. (See Appendix B for details.)

Of course, computers can also be used for maintaining mailing lists, compiling biographical information and "search" information, and creating mailers and newsletters. However, they are serious investments. You should consider purchasing one only if your group intends to be around for awhile, AND if you have someone who is willing to learn how to use it.

Commercial Electronic Networks (Video Tex Industry). These are subscription services that are like huge BBS's, but commercially operated. You pay a one-time sign up fee (sometimes monthly) plus so much per hour for log-on time. Thousands of people belong to these services, and their equipment can handle hundreds of calls at a time. Once inside these databases, you will find hundreds of areas of interest, but so far CompuServe seems to have the only Veteran's interest group, although Summit promises one in January of '89 (see Appendix B). One interesting feature is the ability to have a "live" discussion (on the computer screen) with many different people at once. Messages appear on the screen in the order sent by the people involved in the discussion.

Military Locators. (See Appendix B for Locator addresses.) Each branch of the service, including the Coast Guard, maintains files on all of its active duty, retired, and Reserve personnel. Of course, the big problem here is that most of the people being sought for reunions are "separated," that is: neither active nor retired, but those who simply did their hitch and got out. The records for "separated" and deceased personnel go to the National Archives in St. Louis, MO, and for all practical purposes (or at least, reunion purposes) are inaccessible. Each Locator seems to have its own attitude and policies about dealing with the public. The Army won't return our written inquiries. The Navy, at least, says it doesn't want to respond to the public. The Marines will do it grudgingly, and only if you ask for one or two searches at a time. The Coast Guard and Air Force are happy to help. The reaction to requests from active duty or retired military personnel is definitely more favorable than from civilians. Find someone in these categories to make your request for you.

When dealing with Military Locators, it's a good idea NOT to mention that it's for a reunion. Just say that you are trying to locate the person(s), which is true enough. Also don't use stationery with the word "reunion" on it, and limit your inquiries to FOUR at a time. All Locators have limited personnel and resources, and "reunion purposes" is far down on their priorities list.

If the person you are looking for is not on active duty, the procedure is to write a letter to the person, and to place the letter in a sealed and stamped envelope with the person's name on the outside of the envelope. Also write on the envelope your return address and the words, "Address Correction Requested" (explained on p. 60), in the lower left corner. Send this envelope to the Locator along with a note giving all identifying information about the person in question (see list below), and include the search fee, if applicable. If the search is successful, the Locator will add the person's last known address to your sealed envelope and forward your letter. The addresses of all active duty personnel are available directly.

The above procedure protects the privacy of the individual. You cannot learn his address unless he decides to respond to your letter. And a word to the wise: don't be discouraged when many of your letters are not answered. Not everyone is as enthusiastic about reunions as you.

Furnish as much identifying information as possible, such as:

1. Full name and service number or social security number.
2. Date/place of birth.
3. Rank held at a specific time.
4. Unit in which the individual served and the dates.
5. Individual's job specialty in the service.
6. Name of any decorations received.
7. Individual's place of residence prior to entering service.

The Reunion Schedule

Each day's schedule should be full of activities from about 9 a.m. to after dinner. If you count breakfast, then the scheduled activities can start even earlier. However, some of these activities, especially those scheduled for late afternoon, should be considered "optional" to allow for "rest time." And you might consider a free evening so that attendees can select a restaurant and have a night-on-the-town.

The first and last days are usually half-days, and should not be scheduled for anything important or "mandatory." Anything in the category of "important" or "mandatory" should happen after dinner or right before lunch.

Special committee or board meetings (those not open to the general membership) could take place the morning of the first day before people arrive, or the afternoon or evening of the last day after most have gone home. An early board meeting can help resolve any reunion problems and establish the agenda for a general business meeting.

"Taking care of the spouses" cannot be over-emphasized, especially with reunions that happen on a continuing basis. Showing the spouses a good time is the best way to assure good attendance at your next reunion. This can be done by:

- special name tags and badges.
- hand out pin-on flowers to the ladies at registration or welcoming reception.
- special tours for "spouses only."
- lunch with the mayor's wife.
- special teas.
- wine and cheese tasting.
- shopping trips.
- fashion show.
- special mention or acknowledgement during the program, especially for those who helped with the reunion.
- forming a "spouse's auxilliary."

The following list shows some of the possible activities for your reunion. Please don't assume that you must accomplish all of these. Some are important for any reunion, but others can be saved for future reunions if you don't presently have the manpower and/or know-how. We leave the choices to your discretion.

- check in and registration.
- welcoming reception.
- hospitality time (to get acquainted).
- group photos and social time.
- individual photos/memory book.
- general meeting(s).
- tours.

- continental breakfast.
- memorial service.
- memorial luncheon.
- after dinner dance.
- film viewing: war documentaries, movies and slides of old reunions.
- raffle.
- awards.
- dedications.
- flags and color guard.
- special guests, presentations, speeches.
- membership talent activity.
- professional entertainment.
- spouse's events (see above).
- banquet.
- farewell brunch (breakfast).
- champagne brunch.

Other things to consider:

- Offer an associate membership to individuals and companies who are sympathetic and supportive, but do not otherwise qualify for membership.
- Have imprinted items and gifts for sale at the reunion and by mail.
- Start a history project with group history preserved on film, video, tape recordings or in print. Some groups publish a "unit history" and include individuals' accounts, old photos, etc.
- Have a "war stories" room at the reunion where people can record stories on tape or video, and old photo albums, diaries, uniforms and other memorabilia can be displayed. Also called an "archives room."
- Display memorabilia at the reunion.
- Publish a yearly directory of those people who have been located, and sell it for at least enough to cover printing and mailing costs. Sometimes this is combined with a photo memory book.

- Arrange for RV and camper accommodations at the reunion.
- For professional speakers on military subjects, contact the local public relations office of your branch of the service.
- If you consider your reunion to be "a milestone gathering" or "of national significance," you might apply to the White House for a Presidential "Greeting" (a piece of paper signed by the President). Send complete but brief reunion data to: The Greetings Office, The White House, Washington, DC 20550.

Forming a Non-Profit Organization

Most first-time reunions are the direct result of one person's efforts, or of a small group under the direction of one person. This is really the only realistic way for groups and reunions to start. But once you have had a couple of successful reunions, and you have found that there is a lot of interest and some leadership ability in your group, you might consider forming a non-profit organization. To do so would require that you elect a board of directors, draw up by-laws, state your purpose, and file with your state government. With a non-profit organization, the leadership shifts to appointed committees and an elected board which can be changed with each election. It's very similar to a small business expanding into a corporation. There are two main advantages. One is that it's easier for a non-profit organization to continue if a leader dies or loses interest. The other has to do with eliminating the "personality" or control of one individual or small group that sometimes (but not always!) can get in the way of better things. Also, you will find that, in the long run, more people will volunteer (both time and money) to help a legal organization than a one-person show. This is especially true of new-comers joining an already existing situation. A very fine book on the subject is *Starting and Running a Non-Profit Organization*, by Joan Hummel. (See Appendix A.)

Imprinted Memorabilia and Giftware

An imprinted gift or memento is greatly appreciated and valued as a souvenir of the reunion. These can include group photos and memory books, or imprinted gift items such as coffee mugs, steins, paperweights, playing cards, pennants, T-shirts, caps, bumperstickers, paper napkins, decals, badges, pens, pencils, etc. Baseball caps with group insignias are by far the most popular. If these gifts are made of high quality material, they can also be used as "fund-raisers" by selling them for a few dollars more than they cost.

FORGET HELL!

FIGURE 27. There are many ways to use logos and insignias: stationery, cups, bumperstickers, windowstickers, caps, paperweights, pens, playing cards, plaques, etc.

Reunions

Fourth Armored Division Reunion, April 10-12, 1987, Ellenville, NY. Contact: Harry Feinberg, 53 Washington Ave., Elmwood Park, NJ 07407.

85th QM Co. (WWII 5th Army) Reunion, April 23-26, 1987, Kokoma, IN. Contact: Tom Stewart, 134 West Howard, Galveston, IN 46932.

45th General Hospital Reunion, May 22-24, 1987, Baltimore, MD. Contact: Aaron Grossman, 2280 Burnett St., Brooklyn, NY 11229.

3425th Ord, Co. D, 72nd Quartermaster Reunion, June 12-14, 1987, Villa Roma, NY. Contact: Izzy Goldstein, 158 F Cross Slope Ct., Englishtown, NJ 07726.

H.Q. Co. 28 Infantry Reg., 8th Infantry Division Reunion, June 5-7, 1987, Gettysburg, VA. Contact: Amos Stanbury, 917 Archie, Eugene, OR 97402.

USS Knapp DD-653 Reunion, June 24-28, 1987, Martinsburg, WV. Contact: Francis Wickenheiser, 1109 Pleasure Rd., Lancaster, PA 17601.

Navy

U.S.S. San Jacinto, **(CVL-30),** Apr. 20-26, Pasadena, Tex. Inquiries: J. Lohr, 738 Campbell Drive, Belpre, OH 45714.

135th Naval Construction Bn, Apr. 24-25, Mobile, Ala. Contact: J. Pilkington, P.O. Box 176, Riverside, AL 35135, (205)884-4867.

VP-52/72, Apr. 24-26, Orlando, Fla. Details: L. Wells, 140 Charlotte St., Winter Garden, FL 32787, (305)877-2048.

U.S.S. Alabama, **(BB-60, SSBN-731),** Apr. 29-May 3, Mobile, Ala. Info: J. Brown, P.O. Box 501, Keller, TX 76248, (817)431-2424.

U.S.S. Core, May 2-4, Hot Springs, Ark. Write: H. Middleton, Rt. 2, Box 118A, Cabot, AR 72023.

Ulithi SLCU 34 and ACRON 29, May 7-10. Info: T. Sanderson, 3410 Ten Oaks Drive, Chattanooga, TN 37412, (615)876-9466.

★   ★   ★

35th Div., 137 Reg., Co. H — Co. H will hold a reunion in Ottawa, KS in July, 1987. For more information contact: H. Boohammer, Rt. 1, Baldwin, KS 66006. Tel: (913) 594-6568.

★   ★   ★

The 42nd Rainbow Infantry Division is having its annual reunion in Bloomington, MN at the Radissoa Hotel South, July 8-11. Contact: Reunion Chairman Rube Evanhoff, 5101 West 109th St., Bloomington, MN 55437. Tel: 612-888-2256.

★   ★   ★

L.S.T. 556 is planning a reunion next summer about June. Please contact: Archie Kessell, 115A 17th Street, Huntington Beach, CA 92648. Tel: 714-536-4694.

★   ★   ★

Jerry Corsolo! Where are you? Anyone knowing either fate or whereabouts of Jerry Corsolo, please write to Al Trahar, Rt. 2 - Box 268, Coushatta, LA 71019.

COAST GUARD

USS CAMPBELL (CG W-32)—June 14-16, 1987, Hotel Riviera, Las Vegas, Nev. Contact Norman Rabkin, 11608 Lockwood Dr., Silver Spring, Md. 20904.

USS CALLAWAY (APA-35)—August 1987, Portland, Me. Contact Wallace Shipp, 5319 Manning Pl., N.W., Washington, D.C. 20016.

USS LST 762—Planning reunion. Contact Charles A. Quilico, 914 Caswell St., Fort Atkinson, Wis. 53538.

ALL SERVICES

AMERICAN EX-POWs (Washington/Oregon)—April 30-May 3, 1987, Red Lion (Thunderbird) Inn at the Quay, Vancouver, Wash. Contact Don Barton, 9307 NE Pietz, Vancouver, Wash. 98664.

GUADALCANAL CAMPAIGN VETERANS—Aug. 13-16, 1987, Norfolk, Va. Contact Ted Blahnik, P.O. Box 181, Coloma, Mich. 49038-0181.

FIGURE 28. *The chances of publication are much better if you keep your queries and announcements short and to the point. Here are some examples clipped from magazines and newspapers. There are basically three types: reunion announcements, looking for members (of a group), and looking for individuals.*

CHAPTER 13

Private School Reunions

Working with the School – If You Are on Your Own.

The term "private schools" as used in this chapter means schools that are within the U.S. and not public. This includes secular, religious, and military institutions, both day and boarding schools, and all levels of education from the primary grades through graduate school. Although private school Alumni Directors and Development Offices will hopefully be interested in this chapter, it is written with the same person in mind as the rest of the book, that is: the former student who hasn't a clue where to start organizing his or her reunion.

Working With the School

Unlike public schools, most private schools like to maintain close ties with their alumni because they rely on alumni donations as a source of funding. They will usually help with a reunion, or in some cases do all the work for you because they know there is no better way of keeping up with the alumni than through a reunion.

The first thing to do, even if you are just marginally interested in having a class reunion, is to call the school and find out what they can offer. If you have been on their mailing list, chances are you already have a good idea. Some offer much and some offer little. But you won't know for sure until you ask.

Contact the Alumni Director (or equivalent). If no such position exists, try the Director of Development (the school's fund-raiser). Instead of an Alumni Director, smaller private schools (which would include most grammar schools and some high schools) will usually have a member of the administration or faculty who also acts as a reunion liaison. Depending on the size of your school, there may be additional people who can help you, such as the editor of the school's alumni publication, and the person who maintains the mailing lists.

Some private schools have an all-alumni reunion once a year that includes anyone who ever graduated, attended, or contributed to the school. Other schools concentrate on the "big year" reunions, such as the 10th, 25th, or 50th. Or a school may organize a multi-year reunion covering classes within a five or ten year period. Or maybe an anniversary of the school's founding is coming up which calls for special celebrations and ceremonies, reunions included.

Private school reunions, especially when organized by the school (rather than the class), are usually multi-day events. Activities are school-related and take place on campus. These might include a football game, a tour of new buildings, briefing on new school programs, viewing plans and models for expanded facilities, a religious service on Sunday morning (for church-sponsored schools), receptions and lunches, as well as the big evening dinner/dance.

Large institutions, especially colleges, may organize "regional reunions" in some of the larger metropolitan areas throughout the United States (and even Europe in some cases), inviting all graduates presently living in the area. These are paid for in part by charging an admission fee, but in most cases the school pays some of the expense. The purpose, of course, is to maintain the graduates' interest in the school and eventually convert that interest into donations and bequests. Sometimes the regional reunion is a fund-raising event (or part of one), organized by the school. Publicity is sent out beforehand explaining the purpose of the fund-raising, how much is needed, and that the reunion is part of the fund-raiser. Those who can't attend are asked to contribute. Such reunions are termed "friend-raisers" by some schools, and special bumper-stickers or other imprinted mementos are created to commemorate the event.

The big complaint about school-sponsored reunions, especially the ones that include several different classes, is that they feel "washed-out" — too impersonal. Each individual has the need to feel that his or her reunion has touched them personally in some way. They need to see people they know, and the program must have elements that they can relate to and recognize. Most school-sponsored reunions are simply too vague. The result is not only that people will not return, but that a negative reputation gets built up through the grapevine.

Our advice, whether to a school or to a class reunion committee, is for a "full-fledged" individual class reunion to take place every 10 years. This reunion may or may not be a part of a larger all-alumni reunion—it really makes no difference. The important thing is that the participants get what they need: their own reunion. This will definitely lead to more interest in reunions, and probably to more interest in the school and its activities.

Such a class reunion would have a separate dinner (if it's part of a larger all-alumni reunion), and its own program afterward. The rest of the time it would participate in the activities and program of the all-alumni reunion. Depending on the school, this type of reunion may or may not be organized by the people doing the larger reunion. Most of the time the job is divided up, with the school doing the contacting and mailing, and the class committee taking care of the program and memorabilia. However, we would suggest a little more committee involvement, namely:

1. Provide a "contact" who will take phone calls from classmates inquiring about the reunion.

2. Provide "detectives" to make an extra effort to find missing classmates. (Methods for finding people are discussed in Chapters 6 and 12.)

3. Produce your own mailer or newsletter. (See Chapter 8.)

Some Alumni Offices will help with a "phone tree." This is a great way to build interest if the callers are carefully instructed in what to say and how to say it. "Intelligent enthusiasm" should be the approach. A "cheerleader attitude" is not going to make it, especially with the older alumni. The usual scenario is for several former students who still live near the school to make the initial phone calls from the school's phones. Each contact who sounds interested in the reunion is asked to call others in his or her area, and former classmates that he or she is still friends with. Names and phone numbers are provided, usually by mail, along with instructions on what to say and a list of information and particulars about the reunion.

If you and the school are co-producing your reunion, see Chapter 15 for more tips. It tells how to co-produce a reunion with a commercial reunion organizer, and many of the tips would be the same.

If You Are on Your Own

Fortunately, almost every school can provide some help, even if it's just with mailing and photocopying. But if you find yourself on your own, you can still ask the school for phone numbers of caterers, motels, banquet facilities, and perhaps the Music Department can suggest local dance bands. If your school no longer exists, then you may be faced with organizing a "long distance" reunion from scratch, just like most military reunions. Turn to Chapter 12, "Military Reunions," for more tips.

Most private schools are very interested in keeping up-to-date mailing lists, even if they don't sponsor reunions. In fact, smart school officials regard reunions as a way to up-date the mailing list. So you should be able to work closely with the school in using their lists for your reunion mailers. Since most private schools are non-profit organizations, mailing through the school offices can save a lot of money even if you are charged for it, because non-profit mailing rates are much lower than general rates. If you can convince the school administrators that the reunion will benefit the school (such as including in the reunion fee an amount earmarked for a scholarship fund, a class gift, etc.), they may be willing to do the mailings for you and not charge you for labor, postage, or photocopying.

In picking a date for your reunion, you may want it to coincide with some interesting event on campus. Remember, though, that this may (depending on the event) draw other outsiders to the area. Be sure to reserve a block of motel or hotel rooms early. Some schools have dorm rooms available in the summer when the students are gone. However, dorm rooms, even if cheaper, may not appeal to everyone. It's best to arrange for some commercial rooms, too.

The school's general and/or alumni magazine or newsletter is the easiest way to announce your reunion and request information about "missing" classmates.

For tips on presenting a gift or scholarship to the school, see "Presentation to the School" in Chapter 10.

CHAPTER 14

Overseas American Schools

The biggest problem that we (Reunion Research) have had in advising all kinds of people about all kinds of reunions has been with the Overseas American schools—the schools for the children of military, State Department, Embassy, and corporation personnel and other Americans who were stationed overseas. (Other names are: Department of Defense Dependent Schools and State Department supported International Schools.) The school records are hard to find and harder to gain access to, there is no "hometown situation" to exploit, few publications will accept reunion announcements or inquiries from such alumni, and there are very few current files to search. But lucky for you (if you are an alumni of such a school) because there is now an association called Overseas Brats, run by Joe Condrill, an ex-Army brat himself. And this outfit has its

Joe Condrill of Overseas Brats.

act together, as they say. In fact, it's so together that we don't have to do anything other than turn you over to them.

They have two types of membership (standard and "in-crowd"), a magazine, a newsletter for the "in-crowd" group, an alumni reunion planning guide, a guide for finding people, a yearly weekend seminar for reunion co-ordinators, and if you sign up, you will be informed immediately if your school has a reunion group. What more could you want?

Write for current rates: Overseas Brats, P.O. Box 29805, San Antonio, TX 78229.

There is also a registry for Overseas alumni: The Overseas Schools Combined Alumni Registry (OSCAR). OSCAR has around 27,000 people registered, and close to 200 school contacts. Registration is free; if you expect a reply, include a self-addressed, stamped envelope. OSCAR, P.O. Box 7763, Washington, DC 20044.

CHAPTER 15

Commercial Reunion Organizers

Their Limitations – Working With the Commercial Organizer –
Some Disadvantages.

If you live in a large metropolitan area, the chances are good that
you can find a commercial business to organize your reunion for
you. Why and under what circumstances would you hire such a
business? This chapter will help you answer these questions.

Their Limitations

Most of the people who are in the business of creating reunions
for other people started out by being involved with their own
reunion. For the most part, their interest in reunions is genuine and
sincere, and they are trying very hard to produce high quality
reunions. Their methods of operation, what they do and do not
offer, and what exceptions they will and will not make (important,
as you shall see), vary considerably from business to business. But
being a relatively new phenomenon, they don't have much of a
track record—the next few years will tell us much more.

However, from what we have seen so far, it seems that the
analogy of homemade pie versus store bought pie is a fair one.
Everyone knows that homemade pie is a lot better than store
bought pie. But, still, not a lot of people bother to make pies at
home anymore. Homemade reunions are not quite as endangered as
homemade pies, but in the larger metropolitan areas, some commercial reunion organizers are doing rather well. For example, we
know of one such business that organized 250 reunions during the
summer of its third year of business. Such success must mean that
they are filling a need.

Most people who turn their reunion over to a commercial business do so because they feel that they don't have the time or energy to organize it themselves. This is fine except that we would recommend one more step before doing so: make a few phone calls to see if there might be someone in your group who DOES have the time and energy. Not someone who must be talked into doing it, but someone who has really wanted all along to organize the reunion but has always deferred to others. The point here is not so much that homemade reunions are that much better than commercial ones (however, in most cases they are), but that people should have the right to try their hand at organizing their own reunion. Too often a reunion has been turned over to a commercial company when there was actually someone in the group who would have loved to do it themselves.

However, these businesses will not accept all reunions. They all set a minimum size for the graduating class that they will work with — generally between 200 to 300 graduates. Their "working radius" is usually limited to 100–150 miles from the metropolitan area that they serve, but occasionally they will have a representative in some of the larger outlying areas. If your class meets the minimum size requirement and is located in or near a metropolitan area, you should be able to find a professional business to organize your event (see how at the end of this chapter).

Working With the Commercial Organizer

Reunions are strange social events. They have a psychological and emotional side to them that reaches far beyond first appearances. As a result, many of the complaints that we hear about reunions (and we DO hear a lot because we solicit them) can best be attributed to a feeling of indignance. The specifics are talked about throughout this book: too much of this, too little of that, this should have been different, that could have been changed. But what these people are really saying (and many of them cannot come right out and say it) is that they are indignant. They feel irritated and a little bit angry that their reunion didn't turn out as well as it could have. They actually feel cheated out of what (often retrospectively) they realize could have been an important part of their life. They want (and rightfully so, in our opinion) their reunion to be the best it can possibly be.

With this in mind, you might think that we would have a hard time recommending commercial reunions at all. We would except for the fact that such reunions are easily "fixable" IF the company is willing to make a few exceptions for you. The main disadvantage of a commercially organized reunion can be summed up in one word: impersonal. As we mentioned, most of these businesses try very hard to produce high quality reunions, and in most aspects they succeed. But regardless of how hard they try, they cannot come up with the most important aspect of all: a personal approach. (By "personal approach," we mean the interaction between people who know each other.) If you decide to hire one of these businesses, our suggestion is to let them do what they do best which is anything to do with the business part of the reunion. Then you spend your time and energy with little details that involve personal interaction. The result you are looking for is a reunion with the "impersonal" aspect removed.

So the question becomes how to dress up a commercially organized reunion so that it has the qualities of a homemade reunion. The effect is really not that hard to attain. The basic rule is to have all personal contact (contact between the classmates and the organizers) go through you (or your committee) rather than through the commercial business.

Although this arrangement should be fine with the business since it will save them time and labor and increase their income (by getting more people to attend), you may find that some will balk at our list of suggestions. Some businesses get rather mechanical in their attempt to become more efficient and save money, and, therefore, don't like to deviate from their usual way of doing things. Unfortunately, such an attitude will not help you produce a good reunion. If you can't convince them after showing them this chapter, then we suggest that you do without their services. Your classmates deserve a good reunion. If you don't have the time to produce one, then maybe you should wait a few years until you find someone (in your group or another business) with the time and understanding to do the job properly.

Here is a list of what most of these commercial reunion organizing businesses can do for you:

- rent a facility with a bar and catering service.

- make all deposits and reservations.

- do all the accounting and billing.
- send out standardized mailers and inserts (such as survey forms).
- add a flyer to the mailer announcing the time and place of any additional activity, such as a picnic the following day (however, they will generally not organize this event).
- send press releases to the local radio stations and newspapers.
- make efforts to find "missing" classmates.
- decorate the banquet room with table centerpieces, balloons and/or crepe paper trim.
- make up name tags (usually with photos from your yearbook).
- provide music (usually a DJ, sometimes a band).
- staff the registration table.
- provide a photographer for individual photos.
- provide display tables, slide projectors, bulletin boards, podium, public address system.
- send out the memory book after the reunion.
- give you a print out of your mailing list.

NOTE: The exact details of what a commercial organizing business can and can not offer will vary from business to business. The above list is what can be expected from the better companies. The mark of a good company, as with any business that caters to the public, is that they will provide (or allow for) anything you want IF you are willing to pay for it.

As you can see, these businesses will do much of the reunion planning for you. In fact, the only aspects that they REQUIRE for you to do on your own are:

- the program.
- the memorabilia display.

There is no way that the reunion organizing business can realistically be involved with these aspects of your reunion, although they may be able to provide you with bulletin boards, tables, slide projector and screen, podium, etc.

Many of these companies use the selling point of "you don't have to do a thing," or "be a guest at your own party." Anyone who falls for such an approach probably can't tell the difference between homemade pie and store bought pie anyway, or they don't care if there IS a difference. So, as a result, a lot of these reunions turn out average or mediocre. But the intention of this book is to show you how to produce an exceptional reunion; you can produce a mediocre one without any help from us. And since it IS possible to hire a commercial company AND have a great reunion, then we assume that it's our job to show you how. Here's how:

(NOTE: These tips all focus on eliminating the "impersonal" aspect of commercial reunions.)

- **Use your grapevine.** It's by far the most effective way of finding people, and is the one method the commercial company has the least access to. The commercial company may offer you the moon when it comes to finding people, but the fact is they don't have any magic formula. They are not getting paid enough to do more than one or two searches (per person) through a few databases (maybe even ones that you don't have access to, though it's doubtful), but that's it. If the name doesn't show up, that person is out—they will never find out about the reunion unless maybe a friend tells them. This is where you or someone on your committee must take over. Get the list of "missing people" from the commercial company (after they have had a chance to work on it) and go from there. Chapters 6 and 12 explain all about it.

- **"Personalize" the mailers** that the reunion business will send out for you. Use your own words as much as possible, give an address and some phone numbers of committee members, sign your name(s), include a survey, ask for memorabilia, donations, door prizes, ideas for the program, etc. The best thing, if you have someone to do it, is to have a newsletter (see Chapter 8). By the way, the organizing company will ask that all checks be made out to them and mailed to them. They will do all bookkeeping. Good riddance!

- **Every mailer should have a "missing person" list,** a plea to help find the missing people, and an address to send the information to. Most reunion organizing businesses will be glad to include these in the mailer and provide their own address for receipt of information. However, if the information that they receive back is not specific, that is, does not contain an exact address or phone number, the business will probably not follow up on trying to find the person. Some of the information will be in the form of clues: "To find Joe Jones, ask the guy who owns the grocery on the corner of First and Oak. That's his cousin." Chances are, the business is not going to follow through on such a clue. But it would be easy for you, or someone on your committee, to do. Our suggestion is that all "missing person" information be returned to you or someone on the committee, not to the business. Then you send all specific information (address, phone number) on to the business, and work on the rest. When your efforts result in an address, send it on to the business (have them send out as many mailers as possible since the mailing cost is included in their fee).

- **Have one or two people from your class on duty as hosts to greet the people as they come in.** Most commercial reunion businesses will insist on staffing the registration line. This is fine, especially for collecting money. But it's very important to have your own hosts, too. The people who are arriving are nervous. The first face that they see should be a friendly face from their past. A strange or indifferent face will only add to their confusion. This is the main gesture of hospitality that you can provide at the reunion—and it's relatively painless. One or two people on half hour shifts for the first two hours is about all you will need. All they need to do is greet people and make small talk. If they want something to do, they can hand out name tags. By the way, most commercial companies will have their staff wear name tags that explain that they are not part of the class. This is important in order not to confuse or embarrass your classmates unnecessarily. Make sure (several days in advance) that this is the company's policy. If it's not, ask them to comply.

- **Insist on photo name tags.** Most commercial companies understand the importance of these, but often their name tags are much too small (especially the button name tags). See Chapter 9 for more on name tags. If the company can only provide the small ones, make your own.

- **Have a photographer take black-and-white photos for the candid page in your memory book.** If the professional photographer won't do it, find someone in your group. Sometimes the professional will do it for an additional charge.

- **Dress up your memory book** with biographical information, the statistical results of the survey, an address list (directory), and a letter from the committee.

The following tips are not as essential as the ones above, but only because they take a lot more time and money. Our recommendation is to do them if at all possible:

- They will do one mailing for you. Some companies will do a second at an extra charge, some won't. We consider two mailings to be a better way of of getting everyone involved, finding more people, and getting the interest up. However, the two mailings should not be identical in content; instead, they should compliment each other. See Chapter 8 for a discussion on mailings. If you do a second mailing on your own, see below for tips on how to finance "extras."

- Snacks and refreshments are an important part of a reunion (see p. 129). They give people something to do with their hands other than drink alcohol, the food cushions the effects of alcohol, and the refreshment table provides a natural place for people to meet and "mix."

Financing the extras. Some of the above suggestions may cost you money out of pocket. Your classmates will be sending their registration fees to the company, not to you. How do you get reimbursed? Try one of these methods:

- Ask the company to charge a dollar or two more than they require and turn this additional money over to you.

- Have a raffle at the reunion. You can usually depend on a dollar or two per person by this method. See Chapter 5 for information on how to run a raffle.

NOTE: For tips on how to save money by eliminating certain aspects of your reunion, see p. 39 and p. 128.

Some Disadvantages

- Every one of these companies that we have talked to so far has claimed up and down and sideways that they can produce a reunion at about the same cost as a private committee. There is no doubt that they get volume discounts from photographers, DJ's, balloon companies, and most facilities. But their average cost per person is somewhere between $40 and $50. We know for sure that some great reunions are being produced by private committees for around $25–30 per person in the smaller cities and towns, and $35–40 per person in the larger cities. We haven't collected enough information yet to determine exactly where the discrepancy in these figures lies. We would appreciate more facts and figures here. Please send us your input.

- These businesses prefer the large hotels with convention facilities (Hiltons, Ramada Inns, Holiday Inns, Sheratons, etc.) because they get volume discounts at such places. If you have in mind some well-remembered local place, you may be disappointed. They may outright refuse to deal with such a facility, or charge more than you wish to pay.

- It happens often that a person will want to attend a reunion only if "so-and-so" is going to be there. They don't have so-and-so's address or phone number, so they call the reunion organizers to find out. Most reunion organizing businesses do not have the manpower to honor such a request. If you hire one of these companies, it's important to provide an address and phone number of someone in your class that will appear in all of the mailings, and for you to keep in touch with the company concerning who will be attending. This can get to be a real sore point with some companies who may not be set up to easily deal with such requests. You should thoroughly discuss this with any company that you are considering hiring. Ask them how easily (and how often) they can provide a list of those attending.

*   *   *   *   *

We have heard rumors of people who will organize your reunion for you for a certain amount per person (usually $3 for every person who shows up at the reunion). But so far we have not been able to locate such people to interview about their services. This seems like a rather fair way of doing business, and is certainly cheaper than the other way (described in the rest of this chapter). The chances are that for this price the person will provide only the "business" part of the reunion: making arrangements for the facility, food, music, decorations, photographer, memory book, and maybe the bookkeeping. The committee would take care of the "personal" parts, such as: finding people, sending mailers, and the program. As mentioned in other parts of this chapter, the "personal" part is exactly the part that you should not relinquish. At $3 per person, such a service could definitely be a bargain, depending on the extent and quality of what is provided. But check it out first. Try to attend a reunion organized by such a service, and, at the very least, talk with several past customers to see if they were satisfied.

*   *   *   *   *

Unless you know the exact name of one of these companies, they can be hard to find. The best suggestion is to look in the Yellow Pages under "Party Planning and Services." You will find all sorts of things listed in this section from balloon companies to clowns, but look for a name with the word "reunions" somewhere in the title. If a reunion organizing business is in your area, you should be able to find it by this method. If not, write to us. We may be able to help. Enclose a self-addressed, stamped envelope.

We are always looking for new and updated information. Send us your opinions, experiences, complaints, praises, and recommendations concerning these companies. Also the name, address, and phone number of any such companies in your area.

There are thousands of people and companies throughout the U.S. who cater to the needs of reunions. Among these are: hotels/motels, convention centers, banquet halls, country clubs, restaurants, caterers, balloon companies, party supply stores, musicians, DJ's, photographers, videographers, bartenders, commercial reunion organizers, imprinted giftware manufacturers, trophy and award manufacturers and engravers, art stores, fund-raiser specialists, software specialists, mail order stationers and graphic art suppliers, mail order book suppliers, button and badge makers, historical printout and trivia specialists, clip art and trivia subscription bureaus, and many more. In 1990 we will be publishing *Reunion Organizers Directory,* a yellow pages for reunion organizers, which will list many of these companies. If you would like to be notified of its publication, please send us a post card with your return address. And put us in touch with any companies that should be listed.

APPENDIX A

Sources, Resources, and Bibliography

COOKBOOKS *(See "Fund-raisers" in Chapter 5)*
The following four printing companies specialize in creating cookbooks for fund-raisers and have "how-to" instructions available:

Cookbook Publishers, 2101 Kansas City Rd., Olathe, KS 66061, 800/227-7282, 913/764-5900. Send for their cookbook kit and price list.

Fundcraft, P.O. Box 340, Collierville, TN 38017, 800/351-7822, 800/325-1994 from TN. Send for free fund-raising kit.

Walter's Publishing, Route 3, Waseca, MN 56093, 800/447-3274, 507/835-3691. Send for free cookbook fund-raising kit.

Brennan Printing, 100 Main St., Deep River, IA 52222, 515/595-2000.

The following book is a must for anyone putting together a cookbook:
How to Publish and Sell Your Cookbook, George Beahm, G.B. Publishing, P.O. Box 7359, Hampton, VA 23666.

FACTS, FIGURES, and TRIVIA *(See "Other Embellishments," Chapter 8, and "The Program," Chapter 10)*

Chronologies, yearly histories, old newspapers, and encyclopedia yearbooks (annual volumes) are good for finding interesting facts and figures for mailers, newsletters, and programs. Your local library (reference section) is the place to start looking. Some specific sources are:

The Almanac of Dates, Linda Millgate, published by Harcourt, Brace, and Jovanovich.

Chronicle of the 20th Century, edited by Clifton Daniel, Chronicle Publications, Inc., 1400 pages, newspaper format.

The People's Chronology, edited by James Trager. Published by Holt, Rinehart and Winston, arranged by years, 30,000 entries, over 1200 pages. Especially good.

The Timetables of History, Bernard Grun, published by Simon and Schuster, 700 page paperback. Especially good.

Historical printouts:

Window In Time, 4321 Laurelwood Way, Sacramento, CA 95864. Send your graduation date and get a one page computer printout of the history and other trivia of that time. A real value at $2.50 (1989). You might write first to see if the price has gone up. See "Other Embellishments" in Chapter 8, and Figure 14.

GRAPHICS SUPPLIES AND BOOKS, PASTE-UP TIPS, DESIGNING NEWSLETTERS *(See Chapter 8)*

Dot Paste-Up Supply, 1612 California St., P.O. Box 369, Omaha, NE 68101, 402/342-4221, 800/228-7272. Free catalog. Office Paste-Up Kit is a bare-bones minimum set-up for $60. Also: Lectro-Stix Waxer, $45; Wax Stick, $3; non-permanent spray mount adhesive, $10 per can; paste-up boards; clip art; Post-It Flags; paper clips; colored dots; file card signals; rub-on type; many graphics books, art and graphics supplies. The catalog will give you a good idea of the possibilities in the world of graphics.

The Printers Shopper, P.O. Box 1056, Chula Vista, CA 92010, 800/854-2911, from CA 800/522-1573. Free catalog. Clip art, rub-on type, borders, graphics books, clip art book of humorous certificates, art and graphics supplies, mechanical and electric paper folders, saddle stitch staplers.

Dynamic Graphics, 600 N. Forest Park Dr., Peoria, IL 61614-3592. 800/255-8800. Books (over 70) for desktop publishing and graphic artists, desktop publishing software and desktop art software, 30 minute "how-to" videos on beginning graphics and desktop publishing ($50 each). Free catalog.

Dover Publications, 31 East 2nd St., Mineola, NY 11501. Clip art books. Ask for a catalog of their Clip Art Series.

Graphic Products Corp., 1480 S. Wolf Rd., Wheeling, IL 60090. 312/537-9300. This company makes Formatt, one of the largest lines of cut-out graphic art aids. The product is available only from graphic art stores. However, the catalog, which costs $3 in the stores, is available free from them just for the asking.

Designing Effective Brochures and Newsletters, by D. C. Anema. Kendall-Hunt, 2460 Kerper Blvd., Dubuque, IA 52001. 319/588-1451, 800/338- 5578. $11.95, Visa and Mastercharge accepted.

Complete Guide to Pasteup, by Walter B. Graham, $19.95. One of the best books on the subject. The author is the owner of Dot Paste-Up Supply (above). Order from them.

Editing Your Newsletter: How to Produce an Effective Publication Using Traditional Tools and Computers, by Mark Beach. Coast to Coast Books, 2934 NE 16th Ave, Portland, OR 97212, 503/282-5891. $20.50, shipping included.

Fillers for Publications, 5225 Wilshire Blvd. #304, Los Angeles, CA 90036, 213/933-2646. Subscription packages of filler material for newsletter editors. Clip art, jokes, sayings, interesting information, etc. Cheapest is $68 per year for 12 issues. Ask for free sample issue.

Chase's Calendar of Annual Events, by William and Helen Chase. Apple Tree Press, Box 1012, Flint, MI 48501. Source of ideas, facts, and sayings.

Ink Art Publications, P.O. Box 36070, Indianapolis, IN 46236. Books on printing, graphic arts, newsletters, editing, etc.

The Newsletter Clearinghouse, 44 W. Market St., P.O. Box 311, Rhinebeck, NY 12572. Books and special studies—geared to promotional newsletters.

The Company Editor, by C. Moore and W. Blue. Editing and layout techniques, 200 pages, $32.50, one of the best books on the subject. Available from Dynamic Graphics (above).

Graphic Handbook, by Howard Munce, North Light, 9933 Alliance Rd., Cincinnati, OH 45242. $11.95.

Publishing Newsletters, by Howard Penn Hudson, Scribner and Sons.

How To Do Your Own Paste-Up for Printing, $9.95, order from The Printers Shopper (above).

How to Make Newsletters and Brochures without a Computer, $13.95, order from The Printers Shopper (above).

The Newsletter Editors Desk Book, Arth and Ashmore, $10, Parkway Press, Ltd., Box 174, West Tisbury, MA 02575. 509/693-4596.

How To Do Leaflets, Newsletters, and Newspapers, by Brigham. Kampman and Co., 9 East 40th St., New York, NY 10016.

PHONE BOOKS *(See "Finding People," Chapters 6 and 12)*

If you would like to purchase any current phone book in the U.S., call (800) 551-4400, 6am to 6pm PST. Visa or Mastercharge can be used, or if your local phone company is Pacific Bell or Nevada Bell, the charges can be added to your phone bill. The prices vary per size of phone book. The following phone books can also be purchased through this number:

The Directory of 800 Numbers, Consumer Edition: $9.95; Business Edition: $14.95.

The National Directory of Addresses and Telephone Numbers, published by: General Information, Inc., 401 Parkplace, Suite 305, Kirkland, WA 98033, (206) 828-4777. 195,000 listings, published and updated annually. $49.50 (plus tax for residents of Washington State). This book may be available at your local library (reference section). Among its many listings are the addresses and

phone numbers of:
• Chambers of Commerce of all major cities.
• Conference centers and major hotels of all major cities.
• Important state offices including Information Office.
• County seats of every county in the U.S.

STATIONERY SUPPLIES *(See Chapter 7)*

Quill Corp., 100 S. Schelter Rd., Lincolnshire, IL 60197-4700. Imprinted and plain envelopes; file card trays, metal or plastic, 3 sizes; file cards, 3 sizes, lined or plain and in 6 colors plus white; CopyMaster; address labels.

Walter Drake and Sons, Colorado Springs, CO 80940. For return address labels and imprinted envelopes in quantities of 100.

WINE FOR TOASTS AND RAFFLES *(See "The Program," Chapter 10 and "Fund-raisers," Chapter 5)*

Inglenook Winery, P.O. Box 402, 1991 St. Helena Hwy., Rutherford, CA 94573, 707/967-3300. They offer a red wine (bordeaux blend) entitled "Reunion." Expensive but very elegant looking, it would be appropriate for a raffle or for a meaningful toast involving a small group. It comes in six bottle sizes from the standard 750 ml to 6 liters. The standard bottle is around $30. The methods of acquiring a bottle depend upon your local laws. Wine can be shipped by common carrier (like UPS) from a California winery to a private address in Colorado, New Mexico, Wisconsin, Alaska, Michigan (up to 9 qts.) and of course California. Otherwise, try your local wine merchant or contact the winery for the distributor nearest you. The U.S. Postal Service will not ship alcohol.

MISCELLANEOUS

(See "Finding People," Chapters 6 and 12)
You Can Find Anyone, by Eugene Ferraro. This book will tell you more than you want to know about finding people. The best book on the subject. Available through us—see order form in the back of this book.

(See Chapter 12)
Starting and Running a Non-Profit Organization, by Joan Hummel. University of Minnesota Press, 2037 University Ave. S.E., Minneapolis, MN 55414. $11.95 plus shipping if ordered by credit card, no shipping cost if paid by check or money order made out to "University of Minnesota Press." Phone orders accepted: 612/624-0005, Visa or MasterCard.

Reunion registry for Canadians:
Bruce Haig of Reunion Register sends a list of registered reunions to every daily newspaper in Canada each April. To get on this list send $15 (Canadian) to: Reunion Register, c/o Historical Research Centre, 1710 31st St. N, Lethbridge, Alberta, Canada, T1H 5H1. Phone: 403/328-9011.

APPENDIX B

Sources and Publications for Military Reunions

Contents:
• *List of Publications that Print Reunion Announcements*
• *Military Locator Information*
• *Military Electronic Bulletin Board Services*
• *Commercial Electronic Networks*
• *Other Sources*

LIST OF PUBLICATIONS THAT PRINT REUNION ANNOUNCEMENTS

This is a key to the codes used with the information in this list:

QUESTIONS	ANSWERS
1. Who can use your services?	m = members only
	p = public
2. Do you publish all submissions or on a space available basis only?	a = all
	s = space available
Do you publish:	
3. reunion announcements?	y = yes
	n = no
4. "lost reunion" inquiries? (people looking for their reunions)	
5. "locator requests"? (looking for individuals)	

NOTE: The statements below each address were solicited from the publications by Reunion Research and are printed as given.

"Aerospace Historian"
Eisenhower Hall
University of Kansas
Manhattan, KS 66506-7186

Circulation: 5500
Frequency: 4 times/year
Deadline: 60 days before publication
1: p, 2: s, 3: y, 4: y, 5: y

No charge for a short paragraph notice if sent typed, double spaced. "Aerospace Historian" is the only international journal for aerospace history.

Air Force Magazine
c/o Air Force Assn.
1501 Lee Hwy.
Arlington, VA 22209-1198
703/247-5800

Circulation: 245,000
Frequency: monthly
Deadline: 3–4 mnths before reunion
1: m, 2: s, 3: y, 4: n, 5: n

We accept notices about scheduled reunions submitted from Air Corps, Army Air Forces, and U.S. Air Force active and retired members. We maintain a file on published reunions. If a person is trying to contact someone from a particular unit, we can sometimes be of help with this information.

Air Force Times
Springfield, VA 22159-0180
703/750-8653

Circulation: 99,000
Frequency: weekly
Deadline: Wed. of week before
1: p, 2: a, 3: y, 4: y, 5: y

Our "Locator Service" column runs information about individuals sought, and includes the name, address, and phone number of the seeker. The "Meetings" column refers to upcoming meetings and reunions. Please address correspondence to one of these columns. An Air Force "angle" is preferred, but not absolutely necessary.

All Hands Magazine
Navy Internal Relations Activity
Hoffman 2, 200 Stovall St.
Alexandria, VA 22303

Circulation: ?
Frequency: monthly
Deadline: 5 mths before publication
1: m, 2: a, 3: y, 4: n, 5: n

Will publish announcements from former or presently active Navy units only.

Americal Division Newsletter
Americal Division Veterans Assn.
247 Willow St.
West Roxbury, MA 02132
617/323-2007

Circulation: 2,000
Frequency: bi-monthly
Deadline: ?
1: m, 2: a, 3: y, 4: y, 5: y

Membership in ADVA is open to all officers and enlisted men now serving with or who have served with the Americal (23rd INF) Division. Eligibility includes those who served with Task Force 6814 and Task Force Oregon. Branch of service is immaterial.

The American Legion Magazine
O.R. Dept.
P.O. Box 1055
Indianapolis, IN 46206

Circulation: 2,500,000
Frequency: monthly
Deadline: 7–8 months before reunion
1: m, 2: s, 3: y, 4: n, 5: n

Our magazine accepts notices about scheduled reunions submitted by its members only. Legion membership card number must accompany each submission. The magazine does not have a locator file, and will not give out any information or publish requests to locate individuals.

"AMRA News Report"
American Military Retirees Assn.
69 Clinton St.
Plattsburgh, NY 12901

Circulation: 5,000
Frequency: quarterly
Deadline: ?
1: p, 2: s, 3: y, 4: y, 5: y

Army Aviation Magazine
c/o Army Aviation Assn.
49 Richmondville Ave.
Westport, CT 06880
203/226-8184

Circulation: 17,000
Frequency: 10 times per year
Deadline: 1 month before publication
1: m, 2: s, 3: y, 4: n, 5: y

Files (30,000 names) can be searched. Members only.

Army Navy Union Newsletter
P.O. Box 7429, Stn. A
Canton, OH 44705

Circulation: 5,000
Frequency: quarterly
Deadline: 6 months before reunion
1: p, 2: s, 3: y, 4: n, 5: n

The Army Times
6883 Commercial Dr.
Springfield, VA 22159
703/750-8699

Circulation: 137,000
Frequency: weekly.
Deadline: 3 months before reunion
1: p, 2: s, 3: y, 4: n, 5: y

Address reunion announcements to: "Reunion Editor." If you are looking for someone, address to: "Locator File."

"AUSA News"
Association of the U.S. Army
2425 Wilson Blvd.
Arlington, VA 22201
800/336-4570

Circulation: 156,000
Frequency: monthly(?)
Deadline: 30 days before publication
1: ?, 2: s, 3: y, 4: y, 5: *
(* will forward information)

"Bulletin Board"
Army Sergeants Assn.
1304 Vincent Pl.
McLean, VA 22101
703/821-0555

Circulation: 600
Frequency: 6 times a year

We have not made it a practice to publish reunion and locator notices primarily because of the small size of the publication. We would, however, respond to individual inquiries for locator information. In addition, when aware that a specific reunion or meeting may be of interest to specific members (e.g., former POW meetings), we have made an effort to ensure that the members whom we know fall into that particular category are advised.

"Connection"
c/o Retired Army Nurse Corp Assn.
P.O. Box 39235, Serna Stn.
San Antonio, TX 78218

Circulation: 2200
Frequency: quarterly
Deadline: 1-15, 4-15, 7-15, 10-15
1: m, 2: s, 3: y, 4: n, 5: y

Will search database (2200 persons). Members only.

"Crosshairs"
c/o Bombadiers, Inc.
Box 254
Eagle Harbor, MI 49951
906/289-4440

Circulation: 6000
Frequency: quarterly
Deadline: 3-1, 6-1, 9-1, 12-1
1: *, 2: s, 3: y, 4: n, 5: y
(*see below)

Will be glad to work out a publication exchange policy for any organization having a regularly printed newsletter of military interest, primarily slanted to air force/air crew interest. Reunion announcements printed for reciprocating organizations only. Locator requests printed for bombardiers only. Files can be searched (13,000 names) for donating members only.

DAV Magazine
P.O. Box 14301
Cincinnati, OH 45214

Circulation: 1,200,000
Frequency: monthly
Deadline: 90 days before publication
1: p, 2: a, 3: y, 4: n, 5: n

Send following information: unit, reunion dates, hotel, city and state, and name and address of person to contact.

"Eclipse"
National Assn. of Black Vets
3929 N. Humboldt
P.O. Box 11432
Milwaukee, WI 53211
414/332-5157

Circulation: 10,000
Frequency: monthly
Deadline: 5th of each month
1: ?, 2: s, 3: y, 4: y, 5: y

"Ex-POW Bulletin"
American Ex-Prisoners of War
3201 E. Pioneer Parkway 40
Arlington, TX 76010
817/649-2979

Circulation: 36,000
Frequency: monthly
   Deadline: 1st of each month
   1: p, 2: a, 3: y, 4: y, 5: y

In addition to publishing announcements in the above Bulletin, we can search our files (30,000 records) to try to locate individuals. We need name and branch of service. Name of prison camp, year(s) of internment, middle name, spouse's name, and nickname can be of help. Allow 10 working days for processing. We can be reached by phone: 817/649-2979, M-F, 8-4:30 Central Time. We appreciate SASE, but not necessary.

Comment from Reunion Handbook: This is one of the few military service groups that will search their files for you. Notice that the serial number is not absolutely necessary. If you are looking for someone who you *know* was in a POW camp, this may be the ticket.

"Forward Observer"
U.S. Field Artillery Assn.
P.O. Box 33027
Fort Sill, OK 73503
405/355-4677

Circulation: 4,800
Frequency: bi-monthly
   Deadline: 2 wks before publication
   1: p, 2: s, 3: y, 4: n, 5: n

We publish announcements for field artillery related reunions only.

"Friends Bulletin"
USAF Museum
P.O. Box 1903
Wright-Patterson AFB, OH 45433
513/258-1218

Circulation: 15,000
Frequency: quarterly
   Deadline: 3-15, 6-15, 9-15, 12-15
   1: p, 2: *, 3: y, 4: y, 5: y
   (*see below)

We accept notices for Air Corps, Army Air Force, and USAF reunions. A file is maintained of WWII unit (reunion) contacts for individuals trying find their reunions. We publish all reunion announcements (3), but on "space available" basis for others (4 and 5).

The Jewish Veteran
c/o Jewish War Veterans
1811 R St. NW
Washington DC, 20009
202/265-6280

Circulation: 100,000
Frequency: 5 times yearly
   Deadline: 4–6 months before reunion
   1: p, 2: s, 3: y, 4: n, 5: y

We will not give out members' addresses but we do have an "In Search of" column.

Korean War X-POW Assn.
4801 Goldfield   163
San Antonio, TX 78218

(There is a rumor that this association will search its files for you, but we have no other information.)

"Military"   Circulation: 14,000
2122 28th St.   Frequency: monthly
Sacramento, CA 95818   Deadline: 1st of month
916/457-8990   1: p, 2: a, 3: y, 4: y, 5: y

"Military" is a magazine devoted to WWII, Korea, Viet-Nam and today. Articles are written by the servicemen themselves, not historians. FREE sample copy on your request.

Comment from Reunion Handbook: You can't go wrong with sending a notice to this magazine. Among its readers are people who are deeply tapped into the grapevine of military information and knowledge. Your notice will be read by people who, in their own way (and quite unknown to you), will try to help you and/or pass on the information or request.

"Military Affairs"   Circulation: 2400
Eisenhower Hall   Frequency: 4 times/year
University of Kansas   Deadline: 60 days before publication
Manhattan, KS 66506-7186   1: p, 2: s, 3: y, 4: y, 5: y

No charge for a short paragraph notice if sent typed, double spaced. "Military Affairs" is the only international, English-language, scholarly journal of military, naval and air history, technology and theory.

Natl. Org. of World War Nurses   Circulation: 450
"Newsletter"   Frequency: twice a year
569 S. Main St.   Deadline: 4-1, 10-1
Red Lion, PA 17356   1: p, 2: a, 3: y, 4: y, 5: y
717/244-9132

Location requests must pertain to military nursing personnel.

"Naval Affairs"   Circulation: 160,000
c/o Fleet Reserve Assn.   Frequency: monthly
1303 N. New Hampshire Ave. N.W.   Deadline: 6 months before reunion
Washington DC 20036   1: p, 2: s, 3: y, 4: n, 5: n

Reunion announcements are restricted to sea services only: Navy, Marines, Coast Guard.

The Navy Times   Circulation: 89,000
6883 Commercial Dr.   Frequency: weekly
Springfield, VA 22159   Deadline: 3 months before reunion
800/424-9335 x8636   1: p, 2: a, 3: y, 4: y, 5: y

Navy, Marine or Coast Guard reunions only. Address reunion announcements
to: "Reunion Editor." If you are looking for someone, address to: "Locator File."

NCOA Journal   Circulation: 185,000
P.O. Box 33610   Frequency: monthly
San Antonio, TX 78233   Deadline: 1st of month
512/653-6161   1: p, 2: s, 3: y, 4: n, 5: n

NCOA Journal is a monthly newspaper with a world-wide circulation. Membership is available to all NCO's and Petty Officers. We use reunion announcements as a filler and average about 20-30 per month. No submissions will be
taken over the telephone.

"The Officer"   Circulation: 125,000
Reserve Officers Assn.   Frequency: monthly
1 Constitution Ave., N.E.   Deadline: 30 days before publication
Washington DC, 20002   1: *, 2: s, 3: y, 4: n, 5: n
202/479-2200   (* preference given to members)

"The Officer" is edited for those in the military services, both reserve and
regular, with emphasis upon legislation and policy affecting the Reserve
Forces.

"The Oversea'r"   Circulation: 1000
The American Overseas Assn.   Frequency: quarterly
P.O. Box 7406, Franklin Stn.   Deadline: ?
Washington DC, 20044   1: m, 2: s, 3: y, 4: n, 5: y

We can locate former ARC personnel through our locator file. We do not give
out addresses, but will forward your request to individuals listed in our files.
Please provide a stamped envelope. We publish notices from members, ARC
Overseas personnel, or military units looking for ARC workers who were
attached to their units overseas.

"The Purple Heart"   Circulation: 20,000
c/o Order of the Purple Heart   Frequency: bi-monthly
5413-B Blacklick Rd.   Deadline: 15th of even months
Springfield, VA 22151   1: p, 2: s, 3: y, 4: y, 5: y

"Ranger Register"   Circulation: 3,500
U.S. Army Ranger Assn.   Frequency: 10 times/year
P.O. Box 5823   Deadline: 1st of month before issue
Columbus, GA 31906   1: p, 2: s, 3: y, 4: n, 5: y
404/576-5759

The "Ranger Register" is the official publication of the U.S. Army Ranger Assn.
We publish anything of interest to Rangers and vets, on a space available
basis.

The Retired Officer Magazine   Circulation: 345,000
Reunion Editor   Frequency: monthly
201 N. Washington St.   Deadline: 6–9 mths before publication
Alexandria, VA 22314   1: *, 2: s, 3: y, 4: y, 5: *
703/549-2311   (* see explanations below)

1. Reunion notices from MEMBERS received in the proper format will be
published on a space-available basis. Preference is given to those notices that
affect the greatest number of our members. "Proper format" means: branch of
service, unit or ship name, date of reunion, place of reunion, name and address
of contact person. Please don't send us two or three pages of information about
your group with the reunion information buried in the middle.
2. Addresses of the current members of The Retired Officers Assn. will not be
released, but if information is sent to us in a stamped envelope, it will be
forwarded. Please do not send lists of names. We do not have the personnel to
cross-check our membership with a roster. This service is available to non-
members, too.
3. To find "lost" units, send the information to our Reader Exchange Editor. Fifty
typewritten word limit, subject to editing. Run on a space available basis. This
service available to non-members.

We have a number of addresses for various units and contacts. We will supply
any information possible, or suggest other places it may be found. Please
include a self-addressed, stamped envelope if you expect a reply.

Retirement Life   Circulation: 500,000
1533 New Hampshire Ave. NW   Frequency: monthly
Washington DC, 20036-9853   Deadline: 3 months prior
                                     1: m, 2: s, 3: y, 4: n, 5: n

Reunion items are published once only without charge as a public service for
veterans and retirees of federal agencies to alert them to scheduled reunions.
We will not publish more than one name to be contacted.

"Sea Power"   Circulation: 58,000
Navy League of the U.S.   Frequency: 13 times/year
2300 Wilson Blvd.   Deadline: 5th of each month
Arlington, VA 22201   1: m, 2: s, 3: y, 4: n, 5: n

Only Navy and Marine announcements from members.

"Sergeants"   Circulation: 128,000
c/o Air Force Sergeants Assn. Frequency: monthly
P.O. Box 50   Deadline: 7–8 months before reunion
Temple Hills, MD 20745   1: p, 2: s, 3: y, 4: y, 5: y
800/638-0594

"Thunder from Heaven"   Circulation: 6,000
17th Airborne Division Assn.   Frequency: 3 times/year
62 Forty Acre Mtn. Rd.   Deadline: 1-15, 5-15, 9-15
Danbury, CT 06811   1: m, 2: a, 3: y, 4: y, 5: y
203/748-3958

We publish letters and announcements from our membership or others making
inquiries relating to the Association activities. We respond to all inquiries in an
effort to assist those who are searching for former members of the Division.
Material submitted should be related to Airborne activities and personnel.

VFW Magazine, "Reunions"   Circulation: 2,000,000
34th & Broadway   Frequency: 11 times/yr
Kansas City, MO 64111   Deadline: 6 months before reunion
                                1: m, 2: a, 3: y, 4: n, 5: n

Reunion announcements are published as a free service to VFW members
ingood standing. Reunion announcement forms must be used and can be
obtained by writing to above address. Publication of announcements is limited
to one time per calendar year. We publish all announcements that arrive in our
office not later than 6 months prior to reunion date.

We have not verified the following addresses, but these publications may be
able to help you:

The Stars and Stripes   "Leatherneck"
APO New York 09211   Marine Corps Assn.
                                P.O. Box 1775
The Stars and Stripes   Quantico, VA 22134
APO San Francisco 96503   703/640-3171

The following do NOT publish reunion information or announcements:

Army Reserve Magazine, Washington DC
"Army Echoes," Alexandria, VA
Assn. of Military Colleges and Schools, McLean, VA
"Afterburner News," Randolph AFB, TX
"The National Amvet," Lanham, MD
American Aviation Historical Society Journal, Santa Ana, CA
The Chosin Few, Oviedo, FL
National Military Wives Assn., Arlington, VA

*   *   *   *   *   *   *

MILITARY LOCATOR INFORMATION

The responses printed below were solicited by Reunion Research and printed exactly as received.

U.S. Navy Locator
NMPC 643
Washington DC 20370

"It is not feasible to undertake the necessary research to provide this service even to a limited degree, without serious diversion of effort from normal operating procedures."

Commandant of the Marine Corps (MMRB-10)
Headquarters, U.S. Marine Corps
Washington DC 20380

"Addresses of retired and discharged personnel cannot be furnished due to the Privacy Act and letters cannot be forwarded to last known address due to manpower limitations. When requesting addresses of ACTIVE Marine Corps personnel, the fee is $3.50 each. Make checks payable to: U.S. Treasurer."

Commandant (G-PO-4/42) (officer)
Commandant (G-PE-3/45) (enlisted)
U.S. Coast Guard
2100 2nd St., S.W.
Washington DC, 20593
202/426-1360 (officer)   202/426-8898 or 8899 (enlisted)

"For military addresses of ACTIVE duty personnel your inquiry can be telephonic or written. The Coast Guard does not release home addresses of its prior members. However, we will forward your inquiry to the individual's last known address. The Coast Guard does not charge for this service."

The Army would not respond to our repeated requests for information concerning its locator services. However, here are some addresses:

For Active Duty Personnel:

Commanding Officer   (or)   Commanding Officer
Army Personnel Services Support Center   U.S. Army Enlisted Records
Fort Harrison, IN 46269   Fort Harrison, IN 46249-5301

All Army prior service records are located at:

ARPERCEN
Attn.: DARP-PSE-VS
9700 Page Blvd.
St. Louis, MO 63132-5200
314/263-7774 or 7421

Air Force Locator
HQ-AFMPC/MPCDOO3
Northeast Office Place
9504 IH-35 North
San Antonio, TX, 78233-6636
512/652-5774 (7:30am–4: 25pm, M–F, Central Time)

"This service is provided without charge to any active duty, retired,National Guard, or Reserve service member of their family. Military-related requestors must note that connection so they will not be charged. Public law requires that others pay a search fee of $3.50 per name researched. Checks or money orders should be made payable to 'AFO Randolph AFB.' An annotated list will be provided detailing the status of the individuals on the requestor's list, including such information as deceased, MIA, or retired."

---

*   *   *   *   *   *   *

MILITARY ELECTRONIC BULLETIN BOARD SERVICES

Armed Forces Reunion BBS
P.O. Box 681
Enka, NC 28728-0681
704/667-8021 (data only)

To our knowledge, this is the only BBS dedicated specifically to military reunions and related information. The systems operator is Herb Reith and the board is sponsored by the USS Merrill Reunion Assn. If you don't have a computer with modem, Herb will conduct a manual search if you enclose a self-addressed stamped envelope. Also, reunion notices can be posted manually (send info to above address). A small donation is always appreciated. Make checks out to: USS Merrill Reunion Assn. In addition to over 1400 reunion groups, the BBS also lists helpful veterans organizations, publications, and other military BBS's. On-line 24 hours a day; 300, 1200 and 2400 baud; 8/N/1 or 7/E/1.

---

*   *   *   *   *   *   *

COMMERCIAL ELECTRONIC NETWORKS (Video Tex Industry)

Compuserve is the largest of these Networks with around 450,000 members. Of these around 4,000 check into the Veteran's Forum. Within this Forum are 17 different sections. The one for posting reunion notices or searches for "lost" people is called the "60 day bulletin." Notices will actually remain posted until the reunion date, even if it's longer than 60 days. Ask for their introduction packet.

CompuServe Information Service
5000 Arlington Centre Blvd.
P.O. Box 20212
Columbus, OH 43220
800/848-8199 (ex. Ohio)
614/457-8600

Summit is smaller and relatively new. Their Veteran's Interest Group should be up and running in January of '89. Write or call for prices.

Summit Communications Network
5707 Corsa Ave.
Westlake Village, CA 91362
818/707-9991

Veterans Survival Manual, Ralph Roberts, New American Library, 1633 Broadway, New York, 10019. 212/397-8000.

This book is due out in June of 1989 and will contain a chapter entitled "The Electronic Veteran," which explains about BBS's and Commercial Electronic Networks.

---

*   *   *   *   *   *   *

OTHER SOURCES

The following sources have files or databases that can be searched:

Don Cerveny
5113 Sitton Way
Sacramento, CA 95823

"I have 300–400 units on file of the Army Air Force/Air Corps of WWII. Information often includes association address, reunion committee address, rosters, and unit histories. Include self-addressed, stamped envelope. Donations greatly appreciated; fee arrangement necessary on involved or complicated searches."

Comment from *Reunion Handbook:* Please note that private individuals like Mr. Cerveny are donating their time and energy to make these services available to you. A donation to defray the costs is always appropriate.

James T. Controvich
Army/Air Force Unit Histories
97 Mayfield St.
Springfield, MA 01108
413/734-4856

"I assist unit historians and associations in preparing and locating unit histories. I also prepare bibliographies for Army and Air Force units. I ask that associations forward notice of newly prepared histories to me to keep my files up to date. I also prepare lists of currently available unit histories. My own unit history library is 1500+ volumes and I have access to many 'official' Army libraries. I take telephone calls until 10 p.m. Eastern time."

Service Reunions
3704 Templeton Gap Rd.
Colorado Springs, CO 80907

Run by Capt. Richard C. Knoeckel, USN (Ret). Provides a monthly listing to newspapers, and is currently published in: The New York Daily News, The Arizona Daily Star (Tucson), The San Antonio Express/News, and The Bucks County Courier Times (Levittown, PA), among others. Maintains "Service Reunions National Registry," a database of reunion information now containing over 5900 listings of Navy, Army, Air Force, Marine Corps, and Coast Guard units either currently holding or planning reunions. Will search the database for you. Send for forms to list your reunion or to search for a reunion. $3 donation requested.

INDEX

Letters after page numbers indicate:

m = pages within the Military Chapter.
a = pages within an Appendix.
f = Figures or illustrations.

YOU CAN FIND ANYONE will be the last reference source you'll ever need. Its no nonsense, straightforward approach will take your search from start to finish. Nothing has been excluded. Checklists, tables and illustrations help reveal every method, technique and bit of magic known to the trade.

You'll learn how to:

- *Locate old friends and relatives.*
- *Find missing children and birthparents.*
- *Locate military and government employees, active and retired.*
- *Locate people who don't want to be found.*
- *Locate missing persons for profit.*
- *Use and develop confidential government sources.*
- *Use the I.R.S. and Social Security Administration in any search.*
- *Trace license plates, addresses and phone numbers.*
- *Obtain confidential court and adoption records.*
- *And much, much more!*

- -

ORDER FORM FOR "YOU CAN FIND ANYONE":

Name_____

Address_____

City_____State____Zip_____

Please send me ____ copy(ies) of YOU CAN FIND ANYONE at $13.70 per copy, shipping included (plus 6% sales tax for California residents). Enclosed is a check or money order made out to: Reunion Research.

WOULD OTHER COMMITTEE MEMBERS LIKE A COPY OF THIS BOOK?
OR WOULD YOU LIKE TO SEND THIS BOOK TO SOMEONE AS A GIFT?

- -

ORDER FORM FOR "REUNION HANDBOOK":

Name _____

Address _____

City _____ State _____ Zip _____

	Price	Amount
First book..............................	$12.95	$12.95
Postage for first book...................	1.50	1.50
Each additional book.....................	9.95	_____
Postage for each additional book........	.75	_____
California residents add 6%......................		_____

Total (enclosed).... _____
(Make checks payable to: Reunion Research)

NOTE: We will ship to multiple addresses at no additional
charge. Please enclose an address list. Also, if you are
buying the book as a gift, we will enclose a gift card if
you like. Please indicate how to make out the card, and be
sure that the above address is the one we should ship to.

Reunion Research
3145 Geary Blvd., #14
San Francisco, CA 94118